THE SCHWEICH LECTURES IN
BIBLICAL ARCHAEOLOGY, 1927

THE APOCALYPSE IN ART

THE APOCALYPSE IN ART

BY

MONTAGUE RHODES JAMES, O.M.

LITT.D., F.B.A., F.S.A.

PROVOST OF ETON, SOMETIME PROVOST OF KING'S COLLEGE, CAMBRIDGE

THE SCHWEICH LECTURES OF THE BRITISH ACADEMY

1927

WIPF & STOCK · Eugene, Oregon

Wipf and Stock Publishers
199 W 8th Ave, Suite 3
Eugene, OR 97401

The Apocalypse in Art
The Schweich Lectures of the British Academy 1927
By James, Montague Rhodes
Softcover ISBN-13: 978-1-6667-3495-9
Hardcover ISBN-13: 978-1-6667-9148-8
eBook ISBN-13: 978-1-6667-9149-5
Publication date 9/14/2021
Previously published by British Academy, 1931

This edition is a scanned facsimile of the original edition published in 1931.

PREFATORY NOTE

IN sending forth these Lectures, which were delivered in December, 1927, I feel that I ought to apologize for two things in particular: in the first place for their late appearance, due in large part to the difficulty of getting right the multitudinous details, especially those in the Notes; and in the second place for the absence of illustrations. Nothing short of a separate portfolio of about a hundred pictures would have been of any use; and since considerations of expense forbade this, I decided to have none at all, but to give all the references I could to published reproductions.

In spite of the hope I expressed in my text that my quest for English Apocalypses had been exhaustive, I have to note that one in private hands has recently been brought to light. It is of English execution, and belongs to the Canterbury group. It is a sister book to no. **16** in my list, containing illustrations of the exposition as well as of the text, and agreeing with **16** and **44** in certain irregularities of text. The gloss is in French. Clearly we are not at the end of discoveries, at home or abroad.

M. R. J.

ETON COLLEGE,
Jan. 1931.

CONTENTS

PREFATORY LIST OF APOCALYPSES, MANUSCRIPT AND OTHER

IN each of the three reproductions of illustrated Apocalypses for which I have been responsible—the Trinity, the Douce, and the Perrins—I have given a list of the manuscripts and other monuments known to me. That list must be repeated and supplemented here. I base it as before on the Delisle-Meyer list, which extends as far as no. 57, and in so doing I believe I consult the convenience of students, to whom a settled numeration of items is more valuable than a list based either on chronology or geography, since, to name no other advantages, the addition of fresh material causes no dislocation. Such fresh material is certain to emerge; there must be in the libraries and private collections of Italy, Germany, Austria, Belgium, and Spain, manuscripts that have escaped notice, though for France one hopes that Delisle's research was exhaustive, and England, I really believe, has not much more to offer.[1]

The points which I have uniformly noticed in the brief descriptions of the MSS. are their place, date, country of origin, language and character of text, number and arrangement of pictures: references are given to books in which illustrations or descriptions of them may be found. Certain features which may serve to link copies together are set down, but it will be readily understood that my information is not complete in this particular, nor indeed in several other respects.

Copies of which I have seen the originals or some reproductions are marked with an asterisk.

In spite of the fact that the results of examination are recorded in the text, a little summarizing of them may be useful.

To the *First Family* belong nos. **1–4**, **17**, **67**, **69**, **83** with **44**

[1] But see Prefatory Note.

as a hanger-on: of these **1–3, 44** are English, **4, 67, 69, 83** (Block book) are Netherlandish, **17** is German.

The *half-page picture* copies are nos. **5–9, 11–13, 15, 16, 28, 40, 41, 43, 44, 46, 47, 50, 51, 63, 66, 86, 88**: twenty-three. Thirteen of these are English, the rest French, six clearly following the English tradition.

The following contain a *prose text in French* and have pictures in the text, with two exceptions in which the text is in Latin; **18** (Lat.), **19–27, 29, 30, 38, 39, 42, 48, 53, 58–62, 70, 72, 87, 89** (Lat.): twenty-six. Sixteen are certainly or probably English, ten French.

These have Latin text and *French metrical version*, with pictures at the top of the page; **31–4, 64, 71**: pictures in the text, **35–7**. All are English.

Three copies have *almost full-page* pictures: **10, 45** (with French text), **65** (Lat.): all are English.

Of copies with *full-page* pictures **52, 57, 84, 92** are German: **54** is Netherlandish, **56** Italian.

Anomalous methods of illustration are in **14, 49, 73–5**, all of them French. Also **68** (German): and **89** English.

I have no particulars of **55, 90, 91**.

Cycles not contained in books are **76–82, 85**: three are English, three French, one Italian.

References to pages of the text are added.

***1**. Paris B.N. fr. 403. Cent. xiii. First Family. English work. Pp. 48, 98.

Text in French, with the non-Berengaudus gloss: originally had 94 pictures: 2 are missing.

Half-page pictures except in the Life of John where there are two to the page.

Illustrates Life and Death of John: has scenes of Antichrist. John is bearded throughout: nimbuses are ringed (composed of small rings).

The Witnesses are slain with the sword: there are devils in the vintage-scene: the Lion distributes the Vials.

Reproduced in full by Delisle and Meyer, *L'Apocalypse en français au XIIIe siècle*, Soc. d. anc. textes fr., Paris, 1900.

***2.** Oxford Bodl. Auct. D. 4. 17. Cent. xiii. First Family. English.

Text confined to Latin inscriptions (including short pieces of the Berengaudus gloss) on the pictures: otherwise consists entirely of pictures (92 remain, 4 are missing) two to a page.

Illustrates Life and Death of John: has scenes of Antichrist. The nimbuses are ringed.

Reproduced in full by H. O. Coxe, Roxburghe Club, 1876. P. 47.

***3.** New York. Pierpont Morgan MS. 524: formerly M. le Vicomte Blin de Bourdon. Cent. xiii. First Family. English.

Text and pictures as in no. **2**: but the full text has been added, in Cent. xiv. 83 pictures remain, the rest lost.

Illustrates Life and Death of John: has scenes of Antichrist. The nimbuses are ringed.

Some pages reproduced in Delisle and Meyer, l. c. P. 47.

***4.** Manchester Rylands Library Lat. 19. Cent. xiv. First Family. Flemish copied from English archetype. Formerly Van Hulthem, Didot, Lord Crawford.

Text and pictures as in no. **2**: 96 pictures (complete).

Has Life and Death of John and scenes of Antichrist.

Some pages reproduced in Rylands Library Catalogue of Latin MSS. (James, 1921).

Nos. **1**–**4** are the First Family MSS. used (with the Block-book) by Delisle and Meyer. Others will be found later in the list, viz. **17**, **67**, **69**, **83**. P. 47.

***5.** Cambrai Bibl. de la Ville 482. Cent. xiii. French.

Text in Latin: a large commentary has been added on intercalated leaves.

Pictures 80, half page.

The Beast bites the hand of the Witness: the Lion distributes the Vials.

See E. G. Millar in *Bull. de la Soc. Fr. pour la Réprod. des MSS. à Peintures*, 1924 (hereafter Millar): also Rohault de Fleury, *Saints de la Messe*, and Delisle and Meyer. P. 56.

***6**. Metz. Bibl. de la Ville. MS. Salis. 38. Cent. xiii. French. Closely allied to **44** &c.

Text in Latin.

Pictures: 66 remain, half page.

The Beast bites the hand of the Witness: the Lion distributes the Vials. Islands named.

Pages reproduced in Millar, l.c. A complete set of photographs is in the British Museum, Dept. of MSS., Facs. 57. P. 56.

7. Sold in 1879 by Schlesinger at Paris. Cent. xiv. French: executed for a lady of the family of De la Tour de Pin.

Text in French with gloss: begins with the letter Piissimo Caesari in French.

Pictures 85, half page.

Has the Life of John. P. 55.

8. Namur, séminaire. Cent. xiv. French-Flemish.

Text in Latin.

Pictures 85, half page.

The Lion distributes the Vials: the Kings from the East occur.

Specimen in *Le Beffroi*, iii. 331. P. 56.

***9**. Brit. Mus. Add. 35166. Cent. xiii. English.

Formerly 'Liber domus kalendarum' (a gild of Calenders?): family of Blois in Suffolk: Rev. T. D. Turner of Beccles.

Text, Latin with gloss in red. Begins with Piissimo Caesari.

Pictures 76 (probably 32 are lost: there is a gap of 16 leaves in the middle), half page.

Has a very copious Life and Death of John with the Story of the Robber. The leaves with the death of the Witnesses and distribution of the Vials are lost. P. 54.

***10**. Eton College 177. Cent. xiii. English. Belonged to a nunnery (name illegible): has pictures prefixed which coincide with cycle of paintings formerly in Worcester Chapter house. It is a sister book to Lambeth 434 (no. **45**).

Text in French, shortened, without gloss.

Pictures 98, almost full page.

Has scenes of the Life of John. The Lion distributes the Vials. Described in my Catalogue of Eton MSS. P. 55.

***11.** Paris B.N. Lat. 688. Cent. xiv. ?French: mediocre work.

Text in Latin, with gloss. Begins with Piissimo Caesari.

Pictures 90, half page. Many unfinished.

Has the Life of John. The Eagle distributes the Vials.

Compositions closely akin to those of **66**. P. 54.

12. Paris B.N. Lat. 14410. Cent. xiv. ?French. From the Abbey of S. Victor.

Text in Latin.

Pictures 83 (2 missing), half page.

The Beast bites the hand of the Witness. The Lion distributes the Vials. The Kings from the East occur.

Pages are reproduced in Rohault de Fleury l. c. viii. 55. P. 56.

***13.** Brit. Mus. Add. 17333. Cent. xiv. French. From the Chartreuse of Valdieu near Mortagne (dioc. Séez). Fine work.

Text, Latin, gloss in French.

Pictures 83, half page.

John is beardless. The Beast bites the hand of Witness. The Lion distributes the Vials. The Kings from the East occur.

Pages in Millar, l.c.: in Birch and Jenner, *Early Drawings*: in Brit. Mus. *Facsimiles* (Warner), series 2, etc. P. 56.

14. Chantilly Musée Condé 1378 (formerly in the Westerloo collection). French.

Text, French with commentary. Has Piissimo Caesari in French.

Pictures 83, in medallion form occupying ff. 36–121.

Has the Life of John.

Possibly related to the *Bible moralisée*: the Apocalypse is preceded by an epitome of Bible history illustrated with medallions occupying ff. 1–33. An anomalous copy.

15. Formerly owned by a Dr. Rey. Sold at Tours, June 1920, Colln. of Baron Auvray, lot 203. Cent. xiv. ?English. In 1569 owned by Tho. Darell: and given to him by Rob. Pecham.

Text, Latin without gloss.

Pictures 67 (imperfect), half page: pictures of the Life of Christ precede: at the end are pictures of the owners and their patron saints. In the lower margins are grotesques. P. 56.

***16.** Formerly H. Y. Thompson 55. Sold 1920. Cent. xiii. English, finished in Italy.

Text, Latin with gloss. Closely allied to Lambeth 209 (no. **44**).

Pictures, 76 illustrating text, 76 illustrating gloss: half page. Probably had Life of John (now lost): the Lion distributes the Vials. Islands named.

Pages reproduced in H. Y. Thompson's *Illustrations*, vol. iv, and Sale Catalogue, 1920.

Described by me in H. Y. Thompson's Catalogue. Second series. Pp. 56, 65.

***17.** Brit. Mus. Add. 19896. Cent. xv. First Family. German.

Text and pictures as in no. **2**. The full text of the Book has been added.

Pictures 96 (two to page).

Has Life and Death of John and scenes of Antichrist. P. 47.

***18.** Trinity Coll. Cambridge B. 10. 6(217). Cent. xiii. English.

Text in Latin without gloss.

Pictures 76 remaining: in text. Some directions to the artist remain (see my Catalogue in loc.).

The Lion distributes the Vials.

Described in my Catalogue of Trin. Coll. MSS.

We now have a group of books which contain a French

text and gloss, with prologue beginning 'Seint Pol lapostre'. Other like copies are **58**, **62**, **70**, **87**. P. 65.

19. Paris B.N. fr. 9574. Cent. xiii. ?English. Owned by Blanche de France when a nun at Longchamp. Poor in execution.

Text, French with gloss.

Pictures 68 in text with gold grounds.

Said to resemble no. **20**.

***20**. Lambeth 75. Cent. xiii. English. Moderate work.

Text, French with gloss.

Pictures 70 in text. Described in my Catalogue.

21. Paris B.N. nouv. acq. fr. 6883. French. Poor work.

Text, French with gloss. The volume contains other treatises.

Pictures: few finished. 69 spaces left.

22. Paris Arsenal 5214. Cent. xiv. English. Poor work.

Text, French with gloss.

Pictures in text: number not recorded. The first is of John addressing a group of seated hearers.

23. Paris Arsenal 5091. Cent. xv (2nd half). French.

Text, French with gloss.

Pictures in text largely in grisaille: number not recorded.

***24**. Brit. Mus. 15. D. ii. Cent. xiv. English. From Greenfield nunnery, Lincs. Moderate work.

Text, French with gloss.

Pictures 64 in text. P. 65.

***25**. Brit. Mus. 19. B. xv. Cent. xiv. English. Fine work, partly by the artist of 2 B. vii, Queen Mary's Psalter.

Text, French with gloss.

Pictures 72 in text: white figures on coloured grounds: cf. **60** and **70**. The Lion distributes the Vials.

See Millar, *English Illuminated MSS.*, ii. for reproductions and references. P. 65.

***26**. Brit. Mus. Harley 4972. Cent. xiv. French. Moderate work.

Texts, French with gloss.

Pictures in text: number not recorded.

***27**. Formerly H. Y. Thompson 38. Cent. xiv. French. Collections of Westerloo and Duke of Sussex. Fairly good work.

Text, French with gloss.

Pictures 70 in text: full description in my *Catalogue of Fifty MSS.* (1895).

Page reproduced in Westwood, *Palaeogr. sacra pictoria.*

***28**. Oxford Bodl. Douce 180. Cent. xiii late. Done for Edward I. English. Magnificent work: the same artist illustrated no. **50**.

Text, French gloss prefixed. Latin text and gloss follow.

Pictures 97 (six are missing), half page.

The Letters to the Churches are illustrated: the Beast attacks the hand of the Witness: the Eagle distributes the Vials: the Kings from the East occur.

Has the People rejoicing over the dead Witnesses, the Dragon cast into the earth, the Drunken Woman.

Islands named.

Reproduced in full by C. H. St. J. Hornby for the Roxburghe Club 1922: introduction by me. Pp. 57, 100.

29. Brussels Bib. Roy. B. 282. Cent. xiv. English. Belonged to Charles, Comte de Chimay.

Text, French with gloss. The volume also contains the *Lumere as lais* (or *Elucidarium* in French).

Pictures 73 in text.

Specimen in École des Chartes facsimiles no. 385.

30. Formerly Didot: whereabouts unknown. ?French.

Text, French with gloss.

Pictures 57 (?imperfect) in text.

A group of books now follows containing a Latin text and French metrical version. P. 64.

***31**. Cambridge Magdalene Coll. Pepys 1803. Cent. xiv. English.

Text, Latin and French metrical.
Pictures 89 top of page.
Letters to Churches illustrated.
Full description in my Catalogue of Pepys Medieval MSS. P. Meyer in *Romania*, xxv.

***32.** Brit. Mus. 2 D. xiii. Cent. xiv. English (or N. French). Like **31**, but poor.
Text, Latin and French metrical.
Pictures 102 at top of page.
Letters to Churches illustrated.

***33.** Copenhagen Royal Libr. Thott 89. Cent. xiv. English. Owned in Cent. xv by George Plompton (as Brit. Mus. Stowe 7). Rough work.
Text, Latin and French metrical: a long Latin commentary interleaved in Cent. xv.
Pictures 98, usually at top of page.

***34.** Cambridge Fitzwilliam Museum McClean 123. Cent. xiii. English: from Nuneaton nunnery.
Text, Latin and French metrical: very imperfect.
Pictures, only 21 remain, in outline, at top of page.
Full description in my Catalogue of the McClean MSS.

***35.** Cambridge Corpus Chr. Coll 20. Cent. xiv. English. Given to St. Augustine's Canterbury by Dame Juliana de Leybourne, Countess of Huntingdon.
Text, Latin and French metrical; also French gloss.
Pictures 106 in text.
Letters to Churches illustrated.
Full description in my Catalogue of C.C.C. MSS.

***36.** Toulouse, Bibl. de la Ville 815. Cent. xiv. English.
Text, Latin and French metrical.
Pictures 106 (2 missing?) in text.
Letters to Churches illustrated.
Pages reproduced by Meyer in *Romania*, xxv.

***37.** Brit. Mus. Add. 18633. Cent. xiv. English. Perhaps

from Reading Abbey: formerly Lord Denbigh's. Closely allied to **36**.

Text, Latin and French metrical.

Pictures 106 in text.

Letters to Churches illustrated.

38. Paris B.N. fr. 1768. Cent. xiv. French. Poor work.

Text, French with gloss. Has Piissimo Caesari in French.

Pictures 58 in text.

Has Life of John.

***39**. Cambridge Trin. Coll. R. 16. 2 (950). Cent. xiii. English. Magnificent work: large folio size.

Text, French with copious gloss. The text of the Life of John is here complete in French.

Pictures 89 in text.

Has Life and Death of John, very copious, with the Story of the Robber (as no. **9**). The Beast bites the hand of the Witness: the Eagle distributes the Vials.

Reproduced in full for the Roxburghe Club 1909 with introduction by me. Description in my Catalogue of Trin. Coll. MSS. P. 51.

***40**. Cambridge Trin. Coll. B. 10. 2 (213). Cent. xiii–xiv. English. Perhaps from Westminster: it has pictures of the Life of Edward the Confessor. Moderate work.

Text, Latin with gloss. Begins with Piissimo Caesari.

Pictures 76 remain, half page.

The Lion distributes the Vials.

Described in my Catalogue of Trin. Coll. MSS. P. 55.

***41**. Dresden. Oc. 49. Cent. xiv. French. Owned by the Grand Bâtard d'Orléans. Allied to **6** &c.

Text, French with gloss.

Pictures 70, gold grounds, half page.

The Lion distributes the Vials.

Description and specimens in Bruck, *Malereien d. Hdss. d. Königr. Sächsens*, 1906.

*42. Dresden. Oc. 50. Cent. xiv. French.

Text. French with gloss in Lorraine dialect.

Pictures 72 in text.

Description and specimens in Bruck, l.c.

***43**. Escorial. Cent. xv (1428–35 and 1482). Executed by Jean Bapteur, Perronnet Lami, Jean Colombe for a Duke of Savoy. Fine work.

Text, Latin, with gloss in red. Has Piissimo Caesari.

Pictures? 90, half page.

Has Life and Death of John.

See *Zeitschr. f. bildende Kunst*, 1920, p. 225. (Friedrich Winkler, *Reisefrüchte*, ii), Montaña in *Museo Español de Antiguedades*, iv. 443–83. Durrieu in *Bibl. de l'École des Chartes*, 1893 (liv. 270–4). *L'Arte*, vol. iv (Vesme and Carta). See further in text and notes. Pp. 72, 107.

***44**. Lambeth 209. Cent. xiii. English: done at Canterbury?, owned by a Lady de Quincy. Fine work: allied to no. **16**, and also **5**, **6**. Pp. 48, 56.

Text, Latin with gloss.

Pictures 78, half page.

The Beast bites the hand of the Witness: the Lion distributes the Vials: Islands named.

Pictures of the Life and Death of John, and scenes of Antichrist, from a First Family MS., have been added, as well as many pictures of Saints, &c.

Full description and many specimens in Millar, *Bulletin*, l.c. Described in my Lambeth Catalogue.

***45**. Lambeth 434. Cent. xiii. English: from a nunnery, name illegible, a sister-book to no. **10**.

Text, French, abridged as in **10**.

Pictures 90 (6 or 8 missing), almost full page.

Has scenes of the Life of John. Will be described in my Lambeth Catalogue. P. 55.

***46**. Oxford Bodl. Canon. Bibl. 62. Cent. xiii. English, perhaps from Peterborough. Fine work: flourishing of initials remarkable. Allied to nos. **63** and **86**.

Text, Latin with gloss.

Pictures 78, half page.

The Beast bites the hand of the Witness. The Lion gives the Vials. Islands named.

List of subjects: see **63**.

***47.** Glasgow, Hunter V, 2. 18. Cent. xvi early. French: has the arms of the family of Poitiers. It is the latest of the series. Vulgar work.

Text, Latin with gloss, followed by French prose gloss.

Pictures 48, half page: incomplete, containing only chapters i–xiv.

Description in Aitken Cat. of Hunterian MSS. P. 73.

***48.** Brit. Mus. Add. 38118. Huth bequest. Cent. xiv. French (?Southern). Moderately good.

Text, French with commentary.

Pictures 70 in text.

Specimens in Catalogue of Huth bequest.

***49.** Formerly Huth: lot 232 in sale. Cent. xv. French-Flemish, done for Margaret of York.

Fine grisaille pictures.

Text, French with commentary.

Pictures 78, half page, apparently deviating from the accustomed cycle.

Specimen in the Sale Catalogue. P. 73.

***50.** Paris B.N. Cat. 10474. Cent. xiii late. English, by the artist of no. **28**. Fine work. From the Jesuit College of Lyons: former owner P. de Noalhes.

Text, Latin with gloss.

Pictures 90, half page (4 missing), mostly in outline, a few at the beginning coloured.

Islands named.

Specimen in O. E. Saunders, *English Illumination.*

List of pictures in the Notes. Pp. 59, 99.

***51.** Brit. Mus. Add. 22493. Cents. xiii–xiv. ?English, a fragment of four leaves (3 of chapters iv, v, 1 of xix).

Text, Latin with gloss.

Pictures 8, half page.

Specimen in Vitzthum, *Pariser Miniaturmalerei.*

***52**. Brit. Mus. Add. 15243. Cent. xv. German. Formerly Duke of Sussex. Bad work. Allied to **84**.

Text in German.

Pictures 14, full page.

List of subjects in *The Apocalypse in Latin* (Perrins MS.), James, 1927, p. 45.

***53**. Brit. Mus. Add. 17399. Cent. xv. French. Poor work.

Text, French with gloss.

Pictures in text, number not recorded.

***54**. Paris B.N. néerlandais 3. Cent. xv. French. Fine work.

Text in Flemish.

Pictures 23, full page; one of Life of John, 22 of chapters i–xxii, many scenes in each. List in the Notes.

Letters to the Churches illustrated: scenes of Antichrist.

Specimens in Vogelsang, *Holländische Miniaturen d. späteren Mittelalters*, Strassburg, 1899. Pp. 72, 100.

55. Antwerp, Musée Plantin, MS. 179 (olim. 134) said to be Cent. xv and Flemish.

The catalogue by Denuce (1927) gives few details. The Apocalypse fills 22 folios out of 27.

Text, Latin, apparently without gloss.

Pictures 45 'coloriées de rouge et de jaune': nothing is said of their arrangement, or their artistic merit.

56. Florence, Bibl. Laurent. Ashburnham 411. Cent. xiii. Flemish.

A copy thus described is 56 in Delisle-Meyer's list, but particulars kindly furnished to me show the existence of a quite different book:

Ashburnham 415 of Cent. xiv. has Italian text[1] and 52 full-page pictures, beginning with the Third Seal and ending with the defeat of the Dragon in ch. xix. Not of fine execution, but notable as an Italian copy.

***57**. Nuremberg Museum. Cent. xiv, formerly Weigel's. German. A fragment of five leaves: a copy of **84**.

[1] There is an exposition, referring to the Avignon exile and containing the date 1318. The pictures derive from the Anglo-French cycle.

Text in Latin.

Pictures 10, full page.

Specimen in Weigel-Zestermann, *Anfänge d. Drückerkunst*, 1866.

Here the Delisle-Meyer list proper ends: its nos. 58, 59 are notices of Apocalypses from the old inventories of the Burgundian library and that of René of Anjou. These I replace by existing copies and continue with my own additions.

***58**. Cambridge Univ. Libr. Gg. 1. 1. Cent. xiv. English. Rough work. One item in a large collection of texts.

Text, French with gloss.

Pictures 55 in text.

***59**. Cambridge Corpus Chr. Coll. 394. Cent. xiv. English. Rough work.

Text, French with gloss.

Pictures 69 in text.

Full description in my Catalogue.

***60**. Oxford Lincoln Coll. Lat. 16. Cent. xiv. English.

Text, French with gloss.

Pictures 67 in text: figures in white on coloured grounds as in **25** and **70**.

***61**. Oxford New Coll. 65. Cent. xiv. English. Owner, Domina Johanna de Boun.

Text, French with gloss.

Pictures 66 in text: with many inscribed scrolls.

***62**. Oxford Univ. Coll. 100. Cent. xiv. English. Mediocre work.

Text, French with gloss.

Pictures in text: number not recorded.

***63**. Cambridge Magd. Coll. 5. Cent. xiii. English. From Crowland or Peterborough? Allied to **46** and **86**.

Text, Latin with gloss.

Pictures 78, half page: very fine pen work in initials.

The Beast bites the hand of the Witness: the Lion distributes the Vials: Islands named.

Full description in my Catalogue of the Magd. Coll. MSS. The list of subjects is the same for this and **46**,**86**. P. 57.

***64**. Oxford Bodl. Ashmole 753. Cent. xiii. English. Resembles **31**–**7**.

Text, Latin: French metrical version has been added in part.

Pictures 80, in outline, some missing: mostly at top of page.

Letters to the Churches illustrated.

***65**. Dublin Trin. Coll. K. 4. 31. Cents. xiii–xiv. English. Fine work. To be reproduced in full for the Roxburghe Club.

Text, Latin.

Pictures 73 (2 missing at beginning) almost full page: sexfoils set in square frames. A remarkable copy. P. 62.

***66**. Malvern, C. W. Dyson Perrins 10, formerly Fairfax-Murray's. Cent xiii. English. Very fine work: has resemblances to **9** (and **28**).

Text, Latin with gloss in red.

Pictures 82 (some missing at the end), half page.

Has Life of John. The Eagle distributes the Vials. Islands named.

Reproduced in full: *The Apocalypse in Latin* (Oxford 1927): with introduction by me. P. 64.

***67**. Formerly Sneyd: lot 35 in sale catalogue 1903. Cent. xiv. Flemish. First Family: like **4**, **17**, **69**. P. 47.

Text: inscriptions on pictures (and short text?) in Latin.

Pictures 121, two to page.

Has Life and Death of John and scenes of Antichrist.

Specimen in Sale Catalogue.

***68**. Wolfenbüttel, Aug. 1617. Cent. xiv. ?German.

Text in Latin.

Pictures 57, mostly in the margin; but some full page.

***69**. Brit. Mus. Add. 38121. Huth bequest. Cents. xiv–xv. Flemish. First Family, like **4**, **17**, **67**. P. 47.

Text, Latin, inscriptions on pictures and text on alternate pages.

Pictures 94, two to page.

Has Life and Death of John and scenes of Antichrist.

Specimen in Catalogue of Huth bequest.

***70**. Oxford Bodl. Selden supra 38. Cent. xiv. English. Style of **28** and **60**: contains also the Infancy of Christ.

Text, French with gloss.

Pictures 61 (many missing) in text: white figures on coloured grounds.

***71**. Oxford Bodl. Auct. D. 4. 14. Cent. xiv. English. Belongs to group **31–7**.

Text, Latin and French metrical.

Pictures 99, about half page.

***72**. Brit. Mus. Add. 38842. Cents. xiii–xiv. French. A fragment of 8 leaves.

Text, French.

Pictures 28 in text.

At this point we pass from Apocalypses which are for the most part contained in separate volumes to other cycles found in books and in painting, sculpture, glass, tapestry: but some late comers in the way of separate MSS. are included. Some monuments of later date, or less importance, are mentioned in the text of the Lectures.

*73. Bible moralisée (Toledo, Harl. 1527, Vienna 1179). Cent. xiii. French.

Text, Latin with exposition.

Pictures, 156 medallions illustrating text, 156 illustrating exposition.

Letters to the Churches illustrated. The Beast bites the hand of the Witness: the Lion distributes the Vials.

Reproduced in full by Comte de Laborde, *Soc. Française pour la Réprod. des MSS. à peintures.* P. 66.

*74. Brit. Mus. Add. 18850 The Bedford Hours. Cent. xv early. French.

Text, French rubrics.

Pictures, 152 medallions in border illustrating text: 152 illustrating interpretation.

Letters to the Churches illustrated. The Lion distributes the Vials.

Full list in Gough, *Account of a Missal*, &c., 1794, pp. 56–74. P. 66.

***75.** Cambridge Fitzwilliam Museum 62. Hours of Isabel of Brittany. Cent. xv. French.

No text.

Pictures 139, marginal.

Letters to the Churches illustrated. The Eagle distributes the Vials.

Full list in my Catalogue (1895) of the Fitzwilliam Museum MSS. P. 72.

***76.** Westminster Abbey, Chapter-house, Wall-paintings. Cent. xv late. English.

Text in Latin on paper or vellum sheets attached to the wall.

Pictures, remains of 25 scenes out of an original total of perhaps over 100: probably the Apocalypse occupied the greater part of 6 bays, each bay containing 5 arches and each arch 4 scenes.

Plates in Royal Commission on Historical Monuments, London, vol. i, *Westminster Abbey*, and vol. v. P. 69.

***77.** York Minster. East Window. Painted glass 1405–8. English.

Text, a few scrolls in Latin.

Pictures 81, in 9 rows of 9. The present order is not correct: displacements occur in rows ii–iv, vi, vii.

The Lion distributes the Vials: the Kings from the East occur.

Full list with corrections of order in F. Harrison, *Painted Glass of York*. P. 70.

***78.** Norwich Cathedral Cloister, S. and W. Walks. Cents. xiv and xv. English. Sculptured bosses in the vaulting.

No text.

Subjects about 90.

Full description by me in *The Bosses of the Cloisters, Norwich.* Norfolk Archaeol. Soc., 1911. Pp. 65, 68.

76–78 are plainly copied from MSS.

*__79__. Padua, Baptistery. Paintings on walls and vaulting. Cent. xv. Ascribed to Giusto Menabuoi.

Upwards of 30 scenes: clearly derived from a MS. P. 69.

References to other Italian cycles in wall-painting are in the text.

*__80__. Angers Cathedral, tapestry. Cent. xiv. French.

Originally comprised 84 scenes and 6 large figures: about 15 are missing.

The Beast bites the hand of the Witness: the Lion distributes the Vials: the Kings from the East occur.

Published by de Joannis 1864 and by de Farcy.

Derived from a normal 'Second Family' MS.

List of subjects in the Notes. Pp. 69, 104.

*__81__. Rheims Cathedral. Sculptures. Cent. xiii. French.

Over 60 groups in the voussures of the SW. portal, the W. and S. faces of the adjoining SW. buttress, and the interior of the portal.

Has scenes of the Life and Death of John. P. 68.

*82. Auxerre Cathedral. Glass. Cent. xiii. French.

Eight panels, dispersed in more than one window. They illustrate the Lamb with the Book, the Seals, the Trumpets, the Woman of ch. xii, and John drinking the poison.

*83. Block-book of the Apocalypse. Cent. xv. Netherlands. First Family.

Text, Latin inscriptions on the pictures.

Twenty-five woodcut blocks with over 80 scenes.

Has Life and Death of John and scenes of Antichrist.

Derived from a MS. resembling **4, 17, 67, 69**.

Reproduced in full by Kristeller, Berlin, 1916. Pp. 47, 74.

*__84__. Weimar Grand Ducal Library. Cent. xiv. German. From St. Peter's, Erfürt. The volume has also a Biblia Pauperum. Allied to **52**: **57** is an imperfect copy.

Text, inscriptions in Latin.

Pictures 25, full page.

Reproduced in full by H. v. d. Gabelentz, Strassburg, 1912.

List of subjects in *The Apocalypse in Latin* (Perrins MS.), James, 1927, p. 45.

***85.** Victoria and Albert Museum, S. Kensington. Altar-piece. Cents. xiv-xv. ?Hamburg school.

Text, Latin inscriptions from the commentary of Alexander.

Scenes 45, extending to ch. xvii.

Full list of subjects in *The Apocalypse in Latin* (Perrins MS), James, 1927, p. 40. P. 68.

***86.** Oxford Bodl. Tanner 184 (Auct. D. 4. 16). Cent. xiii. English. From the Peterborough district? Allied to **46** and **63**, but not so fine.

Text, Latin with gloss.

Pictures 78, half page. Has ringed nimbuses.

The Beast bites the hand of the Witness: the Lion distributes the Vials: Islands named.

List of subjects: see on **63**. P. 57.

***87.** Oxford Bodl. MS. Bodl. 401. Cent. xiv. ?English. Rough work resembling generally nos. **19** and **99**, which have the French prose version.

Text, French with gloss.

Pictures 106 in text.

Has scenes of the Life of John. John is beardless. The Ox distributes the Vials. The Kings from the East occur.

***88.** Cambridge Fitzwilliam Museum Add. MS. Cent. xiii. English.

A single leaf of an Apocalypse with Latin text (no gloss), and half-page outline drawings (viii. 3, the Censer and the First Trumpet). A ringed nimbus occurs. John is bearded.

***89.** Norwich Museum. Cents. xiii–xiv. English. Rough work.

A copy of the Commentary of Berengaudus with very

rude pictures, some in the text, some full page. The first is a picture of John writing, the last of his death: he lies in a tomb before the altar. There is a gap after the Third Seal, extending to the angel with the Censer (viii. 3). It is a quite anomalous copy.

A special Note on it immediately follows the List. P. 23.

90. Now or formerly owned by M. le Vicomte de Coussemaker. Cent. xiii.

Pictures 73, on coloured grounds.

91. Now or formerly owned by M. Vander Cruisse de Wazier. Cent. xv.

Pictures 65.

90, 91 are mentioned by M. de Farcy (*Tapisseries de la Cathédrale d'Angers*, p. 13 note) as having been shown at an exhibition at Lille.

***92.** Hamburg, Stadtbibl. in Scrinio 87. Cent. xiv. German. Rough work.

Resembles First Family MSS. in consisting of pictures, usually two to a page: but the text in Latin, inscribed on the pictures, does not agree with that of the First Family MSS. John is beardless.

Specimens (7 pp.) in K. Schellenberg, *Dürer's Apokalypse*, Munich, 1923.

COMMENTARY OF ALEXANDER (see p. 66)

******a*. Cambridge Univ. Libr. Mm. 5. 31. Cent. xiii. ?German: possibly English.

Contains the full text with many gaps: 71 pictures remain.

Specimen in *New Pal. Soc.*, ser. II, pl. 103.

See J. P. Gilson in *Collectanea Franciscana*, ii. 20. P. 67.

******b*. Prague, Library of the Cathedral Chapter. Cent. xiv. ?German.

Abridged text: 83 pictures.

Reproduced in full in lithography as *Scriptum super Apoc. cum imaginibus Wenceslai doctoris*, 1873.

*c. Breslau Univ. Libr. I. Q. 19. Cent. xiv. ?German.

Abridged text: ff. 136, 84 pictures.

Described by Prausnitz in *Zentralbl. f. Bibliothekswissenschaft*, 1921 (xxxviii, 241–7). P. 67.

*d. Dresden: A. 117. Cent. xiv. German.

Abridged text, 62 pictures.

Full description and many specimens in Bruck, *Malereien d. Hdss. d. Königr. Sächsens*, 1906. P. 67.

*e. Victoria and Albert Museum, S. Kensington. Cent. xiv late. Altar-piece with 45 subjects, and inscriptions derived from Alexander. Entered above as no. **85**.

EARLY CYCLES OF APOCALYPSE PICTURES

First Period

I*. Beatus super Apocalypsim (Cent. viii). Earliest dated copy is of 894, formerly H. Y. Thompson 97, now Pierpont Morgan.

Pictures usually upwards of 60, some full page, some smaller.

List of copies in H. Y. Thompson's Catalogue, 2nd series. Specimens of the oldest copy in his *Illustrations*, vol. iii.

See the references to the literature given in the Notes. Pp. 38, 96.

II*. Trèves, Stadtbibl. 31. Apocalypse of Cent. viii. ?Written at Trèves.

Text Latin, largely re-written in Cent. xii.

Pictures 75, full page.

Specimens in K. Schellenberg, *Dürer's Apokalypse*, 1923. A. Goldschmidt, *German Illumination*, 1929, I. pl. 54 and reff. Description given in the Notes. Pp. 34, 82.

III*. Cambrai Bibl. de la Ville, 386. Cent. ix? German? A sister book to II.

Text Latin.

Pictures, full page, 46 remain.

Specimens in *Bull. Soc. Réprod. MSS. à peintures*, 1922 (H. Omont) and see the Notes. Pp. 34, 82.

IV*. Valenciennes Bibl. de la Ville, 199. Cents. viii–ix. German? Had a Spanish owner.

Text, Latin.

Pictures, about 40.

Specimens in *Bulletin* as for III. P. 37.

V*. Paris B.N. nouv. acq. lat. 1132. Cents. viii–ix. German? A sister book to IV but rougher.

Text, Latin.

Pictures, about 40: outline.

Specimens in *Bulletin* as for III. P. 37.

VI*. Bamberg Bibl. A. ii. 42. Cent. xi. Done at Reichenau.

Text, Latin.

Pictures, 50 full page often with two scenes. The cycle is that of IV, V, but the execution is far finer.

Reproduced in full by K. Wölfflin, 1921.

Description in the Notes. Pp. 37, 92.

VII*. Haimo super Apocalypsim, Oxford MS. Bodl. 352. Cent. xii. German.

Nine leaves of pictures with many scenes, prefixed to the text. P. 41.

VIII*. S. Savin sur Gartempe (Vienne). Cent. xi. Wall-paintings in the vestibule of the Abbey church.

Five subjects remain of a cycle originally extensive.

Figured in Prosper Mérimée's monograph on S. Savin, 1845. P. 40.

IX*. Fleury sur Loire. Cent. xi.

The verse inscriptions remain, indicating 18 Apocalypse subjects represented on the façade of the Abbey church.

See Julius v. Schlosser, *Quellenbuch f. Kunst gesch. d. abendland. Mittelalters.*

Subjects specified in the Notes. P. 39.

X*. Lambert of Liège. Liber floridus. Cent. xii. Flemish.

The MSS. (e.g. one at Wolfenbüttel) contain about 27 Apocalypse pictures, some full page. P. 43.

NOTE ON THE NORWICH APOCALYPSE

The Norwich Apocalypse, now in the Castle Museum, belonging to the City Library, and numbered 287, is one of the rudest I have seen, but may be described here, since it is hardly likely to be discussed anywhere else.

It is a quarto book retaining its original wooden boards, stripped of covering: of Cent. xiii late. Text in double columns of 34 lines. All the hands in the volume seem English.

It begins with an imperfect table of chapters to a Canon Law tract in 178 chapters. Then two tables are added (xiv) of the Apocalypse and the treatise *Qui bene presunt.*

Text, the first rubric is—

Inc. expositio prime uisionis in apocalipsim. Beatum iohannem apostolum et euangelistam hunc librum apocalipsim edidisse constat etc.—sequencia manifestant

Apocalipsis ihesu christi—fieri cito

Apocalipsis reuelatio interpretatur. quod reuelationis donum

The full text of Berengaudus's commentary, ending: ut uite eterne participes esse mereamur, qui cum patre etc.

Pictures very rude. At the head of the text John beardless with red nimbus sits face *r.* in a chair, with knife and pen, a scroll on desk.

Pictures in the text: a row of churches, as one building.

Christ throned: 3 candlesticks on *l.* 4 on *r.*, sword across mouth, holds stars. ch. i–iii

two keys, red and silver.

seven stars in a row.

a tree (of life)

a white star

a rod (of iron)
a key
an open double door.
(these illustrate the Vision and Letters)

	Four Elders crowned, in white, seated	
	Four Beasts with scrolls	
	God in vesica holds the book	ch. iv
	an Angel	
	the Lamb with seven horns	v
	Rider with bow	vi
	Rider with sword	
half page	Rider with balances: red ground.	

a gap from vi. 6 to viii. 3, and change of hand

full page in three tiers:	angel with censer, altar	viii
	angel with book, treads on sea and land	x
	John with rod measures the temple	xi
verso, full page	the Woman throned, the sun behind her, the moon at her feet, the dragon below	xii
full page, three tiers:	the Woman on a red beast, with cup	xvii
	an angel flies down: on *r.* and *l.* are six trumpets pointing down vertically, out of clouds.	
	an angel casts a millstone into the sea	
verso:	John and angel	
	Christ on a white horse, sitting sideways: robe spotted with blood: sword across mouth	xix
	angel in the sun: birds on *r.*	
full page, three tiers:	John and angel	xxii
	the same	
	John stands vested before an altar with veiled chalice	

verso, full page: Altar above: before it John beardless lies in green marble sarcophagus: bands of red and blue below.

On a leaf or two following Berengaudus a short tract on Antichrist and some excerpts are added.

The rest of the volume, original, is occupied with the treatise of Richard of Wethersett: Qui bene presunt presbiteri, ending: hic ergo erit consummatus, valete in domino.

THE APOCALYPSE IN ART

I

IN these Lectures we are to consider the history of a particular Book from one point of view, namely, the treatment it has met with at the hands of artists in the centuries between, say, the fifth and the sixteenth. The Book is one to which a previous course of Schweich Lectures has already been devoted. In 1919 Dr. Charles took it for his subject, and his book in its published form must possess an abiding interest for all students who concern themselves with the structure and style of the Apocalypse, even though the Lectures are now superseded by his monumental Commentary. Fortunately for me, questions of structure, sources, and style do not enter into my purview; nor is it necessary for my hearers to know more about the Book as a book than they can read in the Authorized Version of the English Bible. There they have learned, I hope, to see, in the Revelation of Saint John the Divine, something unique. Unique, I say advisedly: for, just as there is nothing like it between the covers of the Bible, so, in spite of the fact that it is but one member of a large class of writings, not one of those writings can hold a candle to it in regard of splendour of vision, yes, and to use a word which has many meanings to many minds, inspiration. You may read its ancestors, its contemporaries, and its successors, *Enoch*, *Esdras*, *Peter*, *Paul*, and be interested, bored, repelled—hardly ever touched. But the living fire of John's Apocalypse has never lost its power to light and warm. The Book which contains the Letters to the Seven Churches, the words about the Great Multitude whom no man could number, which speaks of 'the Lamb as it had been slain', of the Sea of Glass mingled with fire, and of New Jerusalem, the Holy City, with its twelve foundations of precious stones, and the pure river of water of life, clear as crystal—this Book lives.

If it has so close a hold upon our imaginations, who are

critical, who dissect it and date it, now early, now late, who do not read in it a panorama of the history of our time, nor find solace in discovering that the Number of the Beast conceals the name of the person or power whom we most hate and fear, what may we not expect its influence to have been on minds that were not critical? minds of the first centuries, and minds ruled by the unquestioned authority of the Church?

Any one who has looked into the history of the canon of the New Testament will remember that this Book did not immediately win a place therein. Scholarly circles of Christians did not like it. Its style (another unique thing about it), a style whose blemishes are veiled from us by the noble English in which we read it, repelled them. One is tempted to guess that Bunyan's *Pilgrim's Progress* may have been boycotted in genteel circles on its first appearance for like reasons. We even find an orthodox and eminent Roman Christian in the second century writing a polemic against the Apocalypse. But this opposition, I would say, affected the upper circles only. The mass of simple Christians, who from time to time were called to pass through the great tribulation which John foretold, loved it and drew endurance and hope from it. The Church of Lyons, writing of one of its martyrs, Vettius Epagathus, says that he was and is a true disciple of Christ, following the Lamb whithersoever He goeth. The African martyr St. Perpetua, in that wonderful vision which she herself recorded, tells how, when she and her companions had passed into the fair garden of the upper land, they were brought before One who greeted them and passed His hand over their faces. And why? because God shall wipe away all tears from their eyes.

Those Christians of the early centuries who read the Apocalypse most and to whom it meant most were not of those who either wrote much or made great works of art. And those who could pay for beautiful sarcophagi or handsome paintings on the walls of their burial places were not of those to whom the Apocalypse appealed. But even these could not remain unperceptive of the greatness of the Book, and by degrees it took its place with the others that make up the New Testament, and became as proper a subject for representation in the most sacred places as were the events of the Gospel story. When that time has been reached, the material for my Lectures begins to present itself.

For all this has been preliminary. It was necessary to say what I could to account for the vogue of the Book: necessary also to give some explanation of the fact that in the earliest Christian centuries it did not figure in art. But a little more has yet to be said before we can touch the actual subject.

We are dealing with the illustration of a Biblical Book. But the very idea of illustrating such a Book is not an early one. Let me be understood to confine myself to Christian imagery. I do not undertake to survey the subject of book-illustration as a whole. Now in Christian imagery as represented by the carvings on sarcophagi, the paintings in the catacombs, and the gilded glasses, we do not find the carver or painter setting out to portray even the life of Christ as it is told in the Gospels. They confine themselves to a very small selection of scenes, in which the miracles of healing predominate. The artist has not been reading the Gospels and selecting his subjects from them; rather he has depended upon oral teaching and on what he has heard in the services of the Church. When we first find works of Christian art devoted to illustrating a story systematically, it is the Old Testament which is chosen. It is apparently Alexandria which inspires these first efforts: not surprising, this, when we reflect that Egypt is responsible for the first picture-books of any kind that we know.

Not until the sixth century do we find a Gospel book with pictures: and it seems to be the prevailing belief that the two Greek examples which have survived, that of Rossano and that of Sinope (now at Paris) are, like the third, the Gospels of Rabbula at Florence, of Syrian origin.

The bearing of this observation is twofold. First, if the Gospels are not systematically illustrated till so late a date, we cannot be surprised if the Apocalypse has to wait; and, second, if Syria is responsible for the beginning of this systematic illustration, we shall have to look to some other quarter for the illustration of a Book which was regarded with very doubtful eyes in Syria.

We need not then expect to find anything primitive in our material, and the indications so far are that what we do find will not come from Eastern Christendom. But to turn from the negative to the positive. There is in fact a very large mass of works of art concerned with the illustration of the Apocalypse, and it is time that I should proceed to make a preliminary division of that mass.

It seems to me that it falls into three great sections. The first reaches from the beginnings to about the year 1200. The second, from 1200 to near the end of the fifteenth century. The third extends from that date to the present day.

If one must find a label for each period I would say that the first is tentative, the second uniform or standardized, the third eclectic. In the first period there is no main line of tradition. We begin with isolated scenes inspired by the Apocalypse. Then, in various parts of the West, we find attempts to illustrate the whole Book, but these are independent of each other. Geographically, Italy and Spain emerge first; then Germany has something to show. We may find evidence that the tradition of our second period is being formed, but there are many competitors.

In the second period I seem to discern that some one person, a person so placed that his work could exercise a wide influence, produced an illustrated Apocalypse which became the standard for succeeding generations. I think he was not independent of one of the currents of earlier tradition; but, whatever the material was that he worked upon, he breathed new life into it. The thirteenth century sees the apogee of the pictured Apocalypse: it and the fourteenth furnish all our finest examples. I believe that the unknown genius who devised the archetype for our second period was an Englishman, or at least lived in England. England and Northern France are the theatre of the development.

At the close of this period, the illustration of the Apocalypse was again revolutionized by the influence of one man. In this case we can name the man: it was Albert Dürer, whose fifteen woodcuts illustrating the Apocalypse were issued in 1498. He owed very little to his predecessors; but of those who, coming after him, attempted the illustration of the Book as a whole, very few were not dominated by his work. Two main reasons for this can be given: the intrinsic merit of Dürer's work, and the fact that a set of woodcuts was easily multiplied, easily disseminated, and not costly.

But it must be said that in the third period the illustration of the Apocalypse ceased to be either popular or important. Instead of the sets of pictures or the single volumes which treated of nothing else, we have to look for our material in illustrated Bibles which devote but a fraction of their pictures to it. And of the single subjects which caught the fancy of an artist here and there it is really not possible to say much. My survey can legitimately be ended about the year 1550.

However, the first and second periods furnish quite enough matter to occupy all the time that is available.

Of the illustrations which accompany exposition I need only say that it has not been possible to spread them evenly over the whole area. Those shown are briefly noticed in the text: but many details must be reserved for the Notes.

I have labelled the first period as tentative: I have now to justify that epithet.

Long before we can point to any picture representing a definite scene from the Apocalypse, we find conceptions which cannot but be derived from it.

Oldest of all is the symbol Αω. It is not pictorial, but

it is a symptom which cannot pass without mention. Curiously, the very first inscription cited by Marrucchi in his Manual of Christian Epigraphy is this, painted on tiles, in the Cemetery of Priscilla, and possibly as old as the second century: Modestina Α ω.

Next perhaps we must place the representation of the Lamb. But here we are faced by an ambiguity. The Lamb may be chosen, not because it occurs in the Apocalypse, but because of John Baptist's words in the Gospel: Ecce Agnus Dei. And again, a Lamb on an early tomb-slab need not always represent Christ. It may equally well be meant for the Christian, for one of the lambs whom the Good Shepherd carries in his bosom.

We are, however, on firm ground when we find the Lamb standing on a hill. This image must be inspired by the vision of the Lamb on Mount Sion in Apoc. xiv. We do so find Him in the late fourth-century mosaic of St. Pudentiana of Rome, 'the first great Christian religious composition known to us' as Schultze calls it. Here the four rivers of Paradise are flowing from the Mount. Elsewhere we see on either side a group or procession of six lambs, representing the Apostles. This is the case at SS. Cosmas and Damian in Rome (526–30) and in other Roman churches.

In the same great mosaic of St. Pudentiana is the first occurrence of another Apocalyptic image, the symbols of the Four Evangelists, Man, Lion, Ox, and Eagle. These are, you will remember, borrowed by John from the vision of Ezekiel, but with a difference. Ezekiel's cherubims are all four-headed; each of those of the Apocalypse bears but one likeness.

Of such isolated pieces of symbolism, which are among the commonplaces of Christian art throughout the centuries, it is unnecessary to note more than the earliest occurrence. It is more to the purpose to look for a definite scene wholly derived from the Apocalypse. This we find in the shape of the vision of the Majesty and the Adoration of the Lamb in the fourth and fifth chapters. The earliest evidence seems to be a literary one. Prudentius, who died in the early years of the fifth century, has left a set of verses called the *Diptychon* or *Dittochaeum*, which is a series of forty-nine quatrains descriptive of paintings or mosaics adorning the side-walls and end of some basilica. Twenty-four of these relate to the Old Testament, twenty-four to the New. The last, which doubtless describes the subject in the apse or tribune, runs thus: 'The twice twelve seats of the Elders with their bowls and harps, shining with as many crowns, adore the slaughtered Lamb, who alone was able to open the book and loose the seven seals thereof.' This is a quite unambiguous piece of evidence. The Lamb with the seven-sealed book, adored by the Elders, was represented at the very beginning of the fifth century at latest.

We have documentary, yes, and pictorial confirmation of this. Leo I, elected in 440 to the papacy, placed on the façade of the Basilica of St. Peter a mosaic of Christ with the four living creatures, and we cannot doubt that the Elders were there also; for we happen to have a drawing which it is agreed represents Leo's mosaic with one important and historically interesting change. This I found many years ago in a MS. at Eton, a Life of St. Gregory written at the abbey of Farfa late in the eleventh century. It has been commented upon by de Rossi and by Grisar, whose results I use. The upper part of the drawing shows, below, the roof of the portico of St. Peter's, and, above, the façade with the mosaic. In the gable is the Lamb, in a circle: below, the Four Beasts, and below them the Elders in six groups of four apiece, crowned, and holding out their vials full of odours. Our earliest record speaks of the Four Beasts around Christ. Here we see the Four Beasts and the Lamb. How is this? Grisar's explanation is a very interesting one. There is record that Pope Sergius I (687–701) restored the mosaic on St. Peter's, which was partly destroyed. Now, in the Greek Church Council of Constantinople of 692, called the Trullanum, the representation of

Christ under the form of a Lamb was prohibited. The Latin Pontiff would not accept this. It was he, Sergius, who introduced into the Mass, at the moment of the Fractio, the singing of 'Agnus Dei qui tollis peccata mundi, miserere nobis'. What more likely than that in his restoration of the mosaic on the great basilica he should have taken the opportunity of substituting, for a broken figure of Christ, the Lamb, as a further and visible protest against the Eastern attack upon the beloved symbol?

The same Leo who adorned St. Peter's with a mosaic from the Apocalypse placed one of like subject over the arch of the apse at St. Paul's without the Walls. Ciampini (*Vet. Mon.*, pl. 68) shows it as it existed in his time (*c.* 1690), much broken. A restoration of it made after the devastating fire of 1823 still survives. In this mosaic we again see Christ, the Four Beasts, and the Elders. Another record we also have: that Galla Placidia, about 430, in the Church of St. John Evangelist which she built at Ravenna, placed pictures on the walls 'of the seven candlesticks and other matters taken from the Apocalypse'—a record tantalizing in its vagueness. These mosaics are gone, but at least we can still see the Evangelistic emblems on the roof of Galla Placidia's own tomb-chapel.

It can be shown then that by the middle of the fifth century the scene of the great Adoration in the Apocalypse had won a central position in the greatest churches of the West. In the East we look for such a thing in vain. This, however, is a single scene, not a cycle of pictures. With the exception of St. John's church at Ravenna, of which we know practically nothing, no such cycle is heard of before the middle of the seventh century, and that is connected with this country. Bede tells us that Benedict Biscop, Abbot of Wearmouth, returning from his fifth journey to Rome (about 680) brought with him a number of pictures to decorate his church of St. Peter. There were pictures of the Virgin and the Apostles to be placed in the apse, scenes of the Gospel history (and types) to go on the south wall, and 'images of the visions of the Apocalypse of St. John' to adorn the north wall. Clear evidence of a cycle of considerable extent. We are now fairly launched. In the seventh century a cycle of Apocalypse pictures was procurable at Rome. Neither at Wearmouth, of course, nor in any other building do traces of this primitive cycle remain. But we do begin, perhaps within a century of the date we have now reached, to find a cycle embodied in manuscripts.

There is a pair of books containing systematic illustration of the Apocalypse which in my opinion are the best existing representatives of the Roman tradition. One of them is at Trèves (MS. 31 in the Town Library). It has been assigned to the eighth century, but may not be quite so early. The text—consisting of the Apocalypse only—is said to have been a pre-Hieronymian version; certainly it has been largely written over, in the twelfth century perhaps, to make it conform with the Vulgate. Each page of text is faced by a full-page picture. There are seventy-four of these, and one later, added at the end.

The other book is in the Town Library at Cambrai (MS. 386) and is assigned to the ninth century. It is far less complete than the Trèves book, only forty-six pictures having survived. But the correspondence of the compositions is exact. The Cambrai book is either a copy or a sister of *Trèves*.

Only the Cambrai copy is at present accessible, and that but partially, in reproductions. It is highly desirable that *Trèves* should be published in full. But the full notes I have taken of it enable me to describe the system of illustration. We begin with a frontispiece showing an angel addressing John, beneath an arch or pediment, straight-sided, surmounted by a cross and two birds. *Cambrai* here shows more elaborate architecture. This illustrates 'He sent and signified it by his angel unto his servant John'. The next picture is of John and the Seven Churches, 'John to the seven churches which are in Asia'. The third illustrates 'Behold, he cometh with clouds', and not till the fourth do we find the Vision of Christ, with four candlesticks—baluster-shafted—on the left and three on the right, and John prostrate before Him.

In the fifth, we again see John and the Seven Churches; this time each Church has its angel standing by its door. The architecture of these buildings is of course interesting; many of them are domed. The next eight pictures are devoted to the Letters to the Seven Churches, and in them an interesting attempt is made to illustrate the contents of each Letter. Thus, the Letter to Smyrna says, 'Behold, the devil will cast some of you into prison' and accordingly we see a group of five people chained by the hands, and in the door of a building a horned devil seated holding the end of the chain.

Again, in the Letter to Thyatira there is mention of the prophetess Jezebel who is to be afflicted with sickness; 'I will cast her into a bed'; and we see a richly robed female lying on a bed with two candlesticks at the foot. Two pictures seem to be given to Laodicea, of which the second shows Christ standing at the door and knocking.

This habit of illustrating the contents of the Letters is comparatively rare in later times.

But you must not think that I am going to take you through the whole of the Trèves-Cambrai cycle. It is a very full one, numbering, as I said, seventy-four subjects, which compare well with the most usual number in the later books, viz. seventy-eight. Every moment in the Book is illustrated, though sometimes a single picture will cover a large space of text. Thus the four first seals, with the Four Horsemen, make but one picture, and so do three of the Seven Vials: on the other hand, the Lament over Babylon, of which the text is long, fills three pages. To one or two other points I will call attention. The winds, held by the angels that they should not blow on the earth (ch. vii), are curiously conceived. Each is a half figure with blue-winged head, set in a goblet of which the angel holds the stem. Later, we shall see them uniformly as human heads only

The locusts of ch. ix, again, are not monstrous forms but real locusts. The great red Dragon is not a legged and clawed beast but a serpent with six subsidiary heads in a line below the topmost head.

I select six subjects from the Cambrai MS. for exhibition.

(1) First the frontispiece of the angel addressing John. Here the leaf pattern on the arch, the marble column, the birds surmounting it, are all of somewhat antique flavour.

(2) The Letter to Thyatira, showing three moments: (*a*) John listening to Christ; (*b*) John addressing the faithful; (*c*) John admonishing the prophetess Jezebel who lies on the bed of sickness.

(3) The great Dragon and the Woman clothed with the Sun, here standing on the sun and moon.

(4) The people of God leave Babylon and devils come to make it their home. Here is a good sample of the architecture.

(5) The Army of Heaven (ch. xix) above: below, the defeat of the Beast and False Prophet (who has a nimbus). Birds are preying on the slain. The Old Serpent is cast into Hell.

(6) Lastly, a Judgement scene (ch. xx). Note the antique form of the tablet-books with the stylus inserted. Note also the small figure in the centre, whose head and hands are severed. An angel stands by it and bids the severed members reunite. Similarly, another angel beckons to the sea to give up its dead. We shall meet something reminding us of this in another connexion. At present I would have you notice that this Last Judgement is not a conventional one, but modelled strictly on the Apocalypse. And in general it may be well to remind you that the great Last Judgement scenes which figure so largely on the sculptured tympana of church portals, and in fresco and mosaic, are not as a rule based on the Apocalypse, but depend far more on the Gospels and on extra-biblical traditions, and consequently do not enter save by a side-issue into consideration. The angels blowing the last trump, the other angels who

bear the instruments of the Passion, the Virgin and St. John —Evangelist or Baptist—interceding, the Judge showing His wounds, St. Michael weighing souls, St. Peter at the gate of Paradise; none of these constant and familiar features have anything to do with the Apocalypse.

One word more before I leave the Trèves and Cambrai MSS. Their pictures seem to me to be echoes of an early tradition; a tradition originally embodied most likely in books or rolls, as were the earliest Old Testament cycles: though the compositions are such as could be well adapted to wall-painting or mosaic. I look on them as rather degenerate copies of fine and stately originals; and viewing them in this light, I set a high value on them: for me they are (as I have said) the best surviving representatives of a cycle originated at Rome, very probably as early as the fifth century.

I believe you may be more inclined to agree in this verdict when you have considered two other cycles also preserved in MSS. of the ninth century.

The first is contained in three books, a MS. acquired not long ago for the Bibliothèque Nationale (nouv. acq. lat. 1132) at Paris, another which has long been in the Town Library at Valenciennes (these being sister books), and a third known as the Bamberg Apocalypse (A. II. 42 at Bamberg). This was written at the abbey of Reichenau about the year 1000, while the Valenciennes and Paris books are of the ninth century: their text is written in ordinary good Carolingian minuscule; their pictures, a cycle of forty subjects, are completely infantine. The Bamberg MS., with fifty pictures, is a fine work of art, and indubitably represents the same tradition. The pairs of illustrations demonstrating this are taken respectively from the Valenciennes MS. (that of Paris being much ruder) and the Bamberg MS. as reproduced in full by Wölfflin in a publication of 1921. They show (*a*) one of the Letters to the Churches; (*b*) the three angels crying Woe! (*c*) the Woman on the Beast, perhaps the most immediately convincing of all.

It is only recently that I have recognized the relation that subsists between these books. That of Bamberg is no doubt the latest in date; no doubt, also, it represents an archetype more adequately than do its feeble predecessors. Where that archetype was made, who shall say? It stood a good deal below the richer and more imaginative cycle of Trèves–Cambrai, and it does not show the quasi-classical traits which abound in that. The editor (in ignorance of its relationships) speaks of it as rather medieval than antique, and I think he is right.

The other ninth-century cycle of which I am to speak is that of the Spanish MSS. of the Commentary of Beatus of Liebana on the Apocalypse, written about 780. This book was never copied outside the sphere of Spanish influence; it seldom or never got farther than the south-west of France. But in its own region copies went on being made until well into the twelfth century at least. In its standard form it includes, besides Beatus's Commentary, that of Jerome on Daniel. It is very copiously illustrated. Pictures of the Evangelists, a Mappa Mundi (which has been the subject of special study by geographers), Noah's Ark, sometimes pictures of the Life of Christ, are prefixed. Then there are perhaps seventy or eighty illustrations of the Apocalypse, and twelve of Daniel. There may be thirty MSS. of this work. The oldest is apparently that which of late was in the Ashburnham Collection, then in that of Mr. H. Y. Thompson, now in the Pierpont Morgan Library (which rejoices in another early copy). It is dated 894, and was written by a scribe Magius at a monastery of St. Michael for an Abbot Victor. The illustrations selected from it which I show are of (1) the Sixth Seal; (2) the Locusts attacking men; (3) the Fall of Babylon, in which the markedly Saracenic architecture will not escape you; (4) the New Jerusalem. If any of the Beatus pictures has exercised an influence on the books of our second period, one might say it is this. At least there is a coincidence with some of them in the quasi-ground-plan of the city. Or of course we may say that Beatus, however drastically he may have changed the style of his pictures, is really following an older cycle throughout, which older cycle has in due course influenced the later books. I think this not very probable. There is so much independence in the general choice and lay-out of the illustrations that at present I regard them as an original effort. How provincial and barbaric they are you have seen. It may be worth remarking that they reproduce a fashion which we see in the oldest of all Spanish picture-books, the Ashburnham Pentateuch, of besprinkling the pictures with explanatory inscriptions.

Two late members of the group can be studied in this country, one at the Rylands Library, the other at the British Museum (Add. 11695), which comes from the abbey of Silos.

M. Mâle, in his brilliant study of the religious art of France in the twelfth century, devotes a considerable space to showing that the Beatus pictures have influenced much of the sculpture of portals and of capitals in south-western France, notably at Moissac, and even so far north as at S. Benoit-sur-Loire. I cannot here follow out his interesting demonstration: I can only register a word of caution in regard of one of his suggestions. 'Possibly', he says, 'the illustrators of Beatus imitated the pictures of a manuscript from Syria or Egypt.' Pending the emergence of further evidence, I must question whether any such manuscript ever existed.

We now return to more central parts of Europe. I must pass with a mere mention the frontispieces to the Apocalypse which we find in three of the great Carolingian Bibles—those of Charles the Bald at Paris, of Alcuin, so-called, at the British Museum, and of St. Paul without the Walls at Rome: the mosaic, too, which decorated the dome of the destroyed palace chapel at Aix, and of which we have only a poor picture. But I must dwell a little longer upon two French churches which had cycles taken from our Book. One is that of the great abbey of Fleury. We possess only the verses inscribed on this composition, which was placed on the *facies* of the church (whether inside or outside, whether in painting or other medium, we know not) under Abbot Gauzlin who died in 1030. So much of the early portion of the Book is not noticed in these verses that one doubts if they are complete, but as they stand they give eighteen subjects chiefly taken from the latter half, and, as I think, grouped round a large central composition of the Adoration of the Lamb.

The other church is that of S. Savin in the Dept. of Vienne, also of the eleventh century, which has retained a great part of its wall and roof paintings. Among these are relics in the western vestibule of an Apocalypse cycle. These are figured (too smoothly, but adequately as far as composition goes) in Prosper Mérimée's monograph of 1845. The recognizable subjects are: (*a*) Christ in glory, alone (part of some larger scene); (*b*) the fifth and sixth Trumpets, with the Locusts and the Angels in Euphrates; (*c*) the Woman clothed with the Sun; (*d*) Michael and Angels fighting the Dragon.

That, like the Old Testament paintings on the nave roof, these Apocalypse-pictures are taken from a book I have no doubt; but I do not find it possible to assign a date or place to the archetype.

These are eleventh-century cycles. I add a third, from Italy; in the church of S. Elia near Nepi are many scenes from the Apocalypse, of which van Marle specifies the Vision of Christ in the first chapter with St. John prostrate, the Four Riders, apparently some of the Trumpets, and the fight with the Dragon; besides one which he figures, and which is seen to be the Angels holding the Four Winds, which are not heads merely (as is usual) but complete human figures holding long trumpets to their mouths. Here, too, is a beardless St. John looking on, and the Angel with the Seal of God speaking to the other Angels. The rest of the decorations of this church seem to be so much inspired by the mosaics of Roman churches that one may legitimately suppose the Apocalypse pictures to have a like derivation.

Italy has on the whole (after the first beginnings) so small a part to play in this history that I am tempted to add here a note of its few twelfth-century monuments. One is at Anagni Cathedral, also noticed by van Marle. In this the Adoration of the Elders, the Four Horsemen, and the Fifth Seal, with the Souls under the altar, survive.

Another is at S. Pietro, Civate: the description of van Marle allows us to recognize the Woman and the Dragon, some or all of the Trumpets, and the New Jerusalem.

The existence of these eleventh- and twelfth-century cycles in Italy may well, to my thinking, be a survival, pointing back to a lost original of an earlier century in some important basilica.

We find ourselves now in the twelfth century. Apparently—I say apparently, for at any time evidence may be brought forward to upset my present view—there is free trade in Apocalypse-illustration, and those who attempt it are not many.

Of two attempts, some particulars may be given. One is, I think, new: it is from a MS. of the Commentary of Haimo (of Auxerre, it seems, not of Halberstadt) on the Book. The MS. is in the Bodleian (Bodl. 352: 2431) and was written by or for a monk Rudolfus and given by him to a German Abbey dedicated to S. Blaise. The pictures, which are rude enough, are all together on leaves prefixed to the text. After a dedication-picture with S. Blaise, and a full-page picture of Pentecost, one page illustrates the Vision of Christ and the Letters to Ephesus and Smyrna (where there is some attempt to represent the contents of the Letters). The next page gives the other five Letters and the Majesty, with the Elders, the third the Adoration, the fourth the first six Seals: the Fourth Rider is here a black demon: in the Fifth Seal the souls under the altar appear to have stoles and not robes given to them. This misapprehension of *στολαί* occurs elsewhere, e.g. in the Anagni painting and the Bamberg Apocalypse. In the page which illustrates the Trumpets we have, at the Fifth Trumpet, a picture of the Locusts which at first sight recalls the Beatus-picture; but there is no other correspondence traceable. The Harvest and Vintage of the Earth, the Sea of Glass, and the Harpers occupy another page: here the fish in the sea (quite out of place, one would have thought) are rather absurdly prominent. The last page gives John and the Angel, John bidden by Christ to write, the Lamb among the trees of life, and the river of life in front: also John forbidden to worship the Angel, and a group of John, the angel, and Christ. Thus a good many scenes are accumulated on each page. It would be rash to deny the existence of any connexion between this and earlier copies: but the connexion is, to say the least, difficult to trace.

It may be just worth while to note that the unique MS. of this same Haimo's Commentary on Ezekiel, at Paris, has pages of pictures at the beginning rather reminiscent of the scheme of the Apocalypse pictures. They are figured and discussed by Neuss in his monograph on Ezekiel in art.

Of my next example I cannot say that it is a cycle. It is taken from a very famous picture-book of the twelfth century, the *Hortus deliciarum*, of the nun Herrade of Landsperg, which perished with the Strasburg Library in 1870, but which was so much thought of and copied that of its 333 pictures we have records of 228. Herrade did not illustrate the Apocalypse all through: but she may have done more than appears, for at a point where more Apocalypse-pictures might be looked for there was an old gap of two leaves in the MS. The more or less relevant pictures which are recorded are of Antichrist, of the Woman clothed with the Sun, of the Last Judgement, and one other. Now I have collected a good deal of evidence to show that Herrade's models were to a surprisingly large extent, *Greek* illustrated MSS. In the pictures I select this is apparent. First, the Woman clothed with the Sun: a large and impressive figure. Above, the Child is caught away, on the *r.* the Dragon casts down the stars with his tail and vomits forth water: on the *l.* the Beast rises from the sea and smites the saints. And you will note that on his sword are the letters *OAN*, which, I cannot doubt, stand for ὁ ἀντίχριστος. Also that the Dragon is labelled as 'eptazephalus id est septem capita habens'.

Then, perhaps not quite relevant, but, I think instructive, are the three pages of the Last Judgement (evidently representing a large Byzantine composition which Herrade could not compress into one page). They demonstrate two things: the remoteness of the Last Judgement in art from the Apocalypse, and their own Greek origin. On two pages we see the Judge, the Virgin and John Baptist as intercessors, the four-headed Cherubim, the angels with the instruments of the Passion, the throne prepared, the Apostles, Patriarchs, and prophets, and, very notably, the river of fire flowing from before the Judge. Here alike the conceptions of the ἑτοιμασία and the fiery river (derived without a doubt from the Apocalypse of Peter) and the individual figures—notably the John Baptist and the Patriarchs—are all Greek. The third page shows the orders of Saints, and the general resurrection. At the bottom on *l.* birds, beasts, and fishes are disgorging the bodies they had devoured (this detail, again, derived ultimately from the Apocalypse of Peter) and, perhaps most characteristically Greek of all, an angel is rolling up the sky like the volume of a book.

Herrade has another scene which is all but unique in my experience: it is of God wiping away the tears of the redeemed, after which they roam together among the trees of Paradise and the *fontes vitae* like *oranti* in the Catacomb paintings. I cannot doubt that this also is Greek in origin; the palm trees are copied from a skilfully drawn model.

Other twelfth-century cycles there may well be, unknown to me: of one in the Liber Floridus of Lambert of Liége, I do know a little: but, in the only copy I have seen, at Wolfenbüttel, it is incomplete, with about thirty scenes on twelve pages, arranged somewhat in the manner of Haimo.

It is among the documents which give names to the twenty-four Elders, the names being those of the twenty-four courses of Jewish priests.

Upon the whole, I think I may have substantiated my view that though there are symptoms of an authoritative, a Roman, tradition having been formed in early times, that tradition did not dominate Christendom, and that the first period may rightly be labelled as tentative.

II

And now we come to the welter of Apocalypses which fills the thirteenth and fourteenth centuries and dries up in the fifteenth. The last and fullest list of MSS. and other monuments which I have made numbers over ninety items, and I know it to be incomplete. Of some twenty members of the list I have seen neither originals nor reproductions, but even with this deduction the mass of material is formidable. It must now be combed out as far as that is possible.

M. Delisle was the first person who attempted this task; in the introduction to the edition of the French version and gloss on the Apocalypse issued by him and M. Paul Meyer in 1901 he drew one preliminary and valuable distinction. There are, he pointed out, certain MSS. which insert in the episode of the Two Witnesses in chapter xi, some four pictures of the miracles wrought by Antichrist, of his slaughter of the saints, of his setting himself up to be worshipped in the temple of God, and of his being cast down thence by the true Christ. The Scriptural authority for these pictures is not the Apocalypse, but the second Epistle to the Thessalonians, in which St. Paul speaks of the Man of Sin who is to work lying wonders, and sit in the temple of God, showing himself that he is God, whom the Lord shall consume with the breath of His mouth and destroy with the brightness of His coming.

The MSS. which contain these pictures M. Delisle designates as the First Family. These MSS. also agree in prefixing and affixing to the Book a pictured Life and Death of St. John (though in this they do not stand alone). The large majority of them also consist entirely of pictures, with such text as there is written in the field of the pictures. In fact, only one out of a total of seven (or at a pinch eight) has a full text and gloss on the same page as the pictures.

There are enough peculiarities here to make the isolation of this group easy. But when we come to examine the large mass of copies which have been lumped together under the name of the Second Family the task of discrimination is far more complicated. There are many subdivisions and there are many cross-divisions: I may say at once that I consider it impossible to draw up such a pedigree as can be constructed for a classical text. The best that I can do is to indicate the subgroups which seem to emerge from the mass.

We have two main elements to consider—text and pictures: and one line of demarcation which ought to be helpful is afforded by the character of the text. Is it in Latin or French? does it consist of the text of the Book alone, or has it a commentary? if so, what commentary? is it in prose or verse?

One common type shows a Latin text with a gloss consisting of extracts from the Commentary of Berengaudus, a ninth-century writer: seventeen copies at least have this in Latin. Another group has a French text and gloss derived from Berengaudus. A third has a French text and gloss not derived from Berengaudus: it is this which Delisle and Meyer have edited: eighteen pictured copies and others which have no pictures contain it.[1]

[1] The Berengaudus gloss in Latin begins:

Apocalipsis reuelatio interpretatur

and in French:

Apocalipse signefie demustrance

The non-Berengaudus gloss in French begins:

Par seint Johan sunt signefie li bon prelat

A fourth group has a French metrical version, sometimes coupled with a prose text (Latin or French). This metrical version was made in England. A group at present confined to two members has a shortened prose text without gloss, in French: and a not large group has the Latin text without gloss: while, in isolated copies, commentaries of considerable length have been added, either in Latin or French.

Those are the main facts about the text. What of the pictures in these Second Family MSS.? Numerically there is something like equality of division between two fashions (say twenty-six of each kind): one of placing the pictures anywhere on the page, and varying them in size. This includes nearly all those that have a French version either in prose or in metre. The other, of setting a half-page picture at the top of each page and writing the text, and gloss, if any, in double columns below it. Very nearly all the best copies conform to this system. An exception is made by one of the very finest of all, at Trinity College, Cambridge: but its page is unwontedly large and its gloss unwontedly copious: facts which I think must have influenced the arrangement. Other copies of equally early date have the half-page system. Very few—six or seven perhaps—have full or nearly full-page pictures, and several of these are otherwise eccentric in plan.

On the whole, we may say that two considerable groups emerge, the half-page copies and the French version (metrical or prose) copies, and that the half-page copies are the standard form.

Of these half-page copies ten are clearly English, seven clearly French: of others I have insufficient knowledge.

Of the French-version copies twenty-two are clearly English, and only three clearly French. Thus in both classes there is a preponderance of English influence; and in that connexion it has to be said that six of the clearly French half-page examples are copied from one particular type of English book. One particular type: for you can readily imagine that when we begin examining even a superficially uniform group like the English half-page copies, we find marked varieties among them. But upon that matter I must not enter yet.

Minutiae of detail are inevitable: the subject demands them, and the time for them is approaching. What I have so far been laying before you, I do not reckon as minute detail, but rather as outline. I have tried to describe the character of the Families, but only quite broadly, and to give you an idea of the extent and variety of the Second. We shall now return to the First, and really indulge in some detail about it.

I have said that these books form a clearly marked group, distinguished by their pictures of Antichrist. We have now to inquire of what that group consists. At present I make out seven members of it, and an eighth on the borderline. The three oldest copies are English, of the thirteenth century. The rest are Flemish or German of the fourteenth: none is French, a noteworthy point.

With one exception the seven are uniform in their lay-out, being purely picture-books with descriptive legends written on the pictures. These legends are in the main from the text of the Book, but include short pieces of the Berengaudus gloss. The copies, numbered according to my Prefatory List, are:

2. Bodleian Auct. D. 4. 17 which was reproduced in full for the Roxburghe Club in 1876.

3. A copy now in the Pierpont Morgan library formerly owned by the Vicomte Blin de Bourdon.

These are closely allied in date and style and are English.

4, 67, 69. Three Flemish copies of an exactly similar archetype: one in the Rylands Library, one formerly in the Sneyd Collection, then Mr. Fairfax-Murray's, and one in the British Museum (Add. 38121) from the Huth Library. These are of the fourteenth century.

17. A fourth which I call German, also of the fourteenth century, is in the British Museum (Add. 19896).

83. Uniform with these is the well-known Block-book of the

Apocalypse, now best accessible in the recent reproduction by Dr. Kristeller. This of course is of the fifteenth century and hails from the Low Countries.

1. An exception is the Paris MS. B.N. fr. 403, a thirteenth-century English book, reproduced in full by Delisle and Meyer. This is a half-page copy with French text and gloss—the non-Berengaudus gloss. It was acquired for France probably under Charles V. In the fifteenth century it came back to England with John, Duke of Bedford, passed to a Flemish collector, Louis de Bruges, lord of La Gruythuyse, and finally settled in France under Louis XII.

The group, you see, is a small one, and but for the accident of a copy having made its way to the Low Countries and having been multiplied there in manuscript and xylography, it would have been smaller still.

44, 54. It has a couple of hangers-on which are worth mentioning. A Lambeth MS. (209), otherwise of the Second Family, has had the Antichrist pictures inserted into its margins, and pictures of the Life and Death of John added at the end: both from a First Family MS. It ranks as the eighth of my group. And a Netherlandish MS. at Paris (of which more will be said), deriving on the whole from the Second Family, has used the Antichrist scenes in one of its compositions.

Returning to the group proper, we take stock of its main features. Prefixed to the Apocalypse are certain scenes from the life of St. John derived ultimately from the Apocryphal Acts of John, which were written about the middle of the second century, and which, gradually purged of the unorthodox doctrine of which they were the vehicle, made their way into the service books of the Church in the form of Legends or Lessons read on the feast day of the saint, as well as into such popular works as the *Legenda Aurea.* These scenes represent St. John preaching to the heathen at Ephesus, baptizing a convert (a lady named Drusiana), complained of to the Proconsul or Provost of Ephesus, sent by him to Rome to Domitian; by Domitian he is put into a cauldron of boiling oil which does him no harm, and is then banished to Patmos. Then follow about seventy-eight pictures illustrating the Apocalypse itself; then the sequel of the story of St. John, in which we first see him returning from exile to Ephesus; then raising from the dead his former convert Drusiana. On this follows a story of his changing sticks and stones into gold and jewels for the benefit of two youths who had given up all their property and then repented of it. This story is told completely in very few of the MSS.: it should end with another change of mind in the young men, and the changing back of the gold and jewels into sticks and stones. Next we have the temple of Artemis falling down at St. John's word, then St. John drinking poison without hurt, and lastly the scene of his ordering a grave to be dug for him, lying down in it, and giving up the ghost. The presence of this second set of scenes is a mark of the First Family MSS. and of a very few of the Second Family, whereas some of the Second Family copies have the first set of scenes alone.

We further note certain technical peculiarities in the First Family copies, the English ones more especially. The grounds of the pictures are always left plain: the colouring of draperies, &c. is not full; it is rather tinting and washing; and the nimbuses are not drawn as continuous circles round the head, but are shown as a circle of tiny rings. These peculiarities have been observed to link up the Apocalypses which contain them with certain other books which can be assigned to a definite home. These other books are connected with the abbey of St. Albans, and with the name of Matthew Paris, historian and artist. They are Lives of Saints—St. Alban, St. Thomas of Canterbury, Edward the Confessor—and of the founder of St. Albans, King Offa, and a mythical predecessor of the same name. They are all picture-books with half-page pictures washed with colour on plain grounds, and where nimbuses occur they are ringed nimbuses. Besides, there is very marked similarity in composition and in details, such as ships. I am led therefore to christen our First Family Apocalypses the St. Albans group, and to believe that this type of Apocalypse originated at St. Albans. No one has as yet found a more plausible attribution.

We have now to examine the illustrations of the Apocalypse which this group offers, and note what is characteristic in them. There is no attempt to deal with the Letters to the Seven Churches. The Churches are shown in one picture, along with the Vision of Christ among the candlesticks. At the opening of the Fourth Seal the Rider on the Pale Horse carries a bowl of fire in his hand. Passing on to the eleventh chapter, we find an important mark of difference. Not only, as we know, are there scenes of Antichrist's doings and of his fall, but the death of the Two Witnesses is shown in a particular way: they are beheaded in the presence of Antichrist, who is a purely human figure. Elsewhere, we shall see, the Beast, a monstrous four-legged form in a mail shirt, is trampling on their bodies and crushing the hand of one of them in his jaws.

In the fourteenth chapter we see the Vintage of the Earth trodden out. Those who tread it in the vat are devils. In the fifteenth, when the Seven Vials are delivered to the Angels, the one of the Four Beasts who distributes them is the Lion.

In chapter xx the final defeat of the Beast or Devil is followed by a picture of a large Hell mouth. The last scene that illustrates the text is of John adoring Christ.

Several of these features recur in members of the Second Family, but for one reason or another I have thought all of them worth mention here.

Examples of the First Family MSS:

1. Two pages from the Blin de Bourdon-Morgan MS.: the pictures of Antichrist.

i. *a*. The Two Witnesses are beheaded in the presence of Antichrist.

b. Antichrist's miracles, which here consist in making trees uproot themselves, and their roots to bear leaves and branches. Those who reject him are slain.

ii. *a*. Antichrist sits in the Temple as God. Those who accept him are rewarded; others are slain.

b. Christ casts down fire upon him, and devils drag him from his throne: outside, his followers lament.

2. The same scenes from the Lambeth MS. 209, where they have been inserted in the lower margins of pages, and some figures have been omitted from lack of space.

3. Pages from the Paris MS. B.N. fr. 403.

i. The Angels holding the Four Winds (chapter vii). The representation of the Winds as four human heads held by the Angel is not very unlike that in the Trèves MS. It runs through all the copies until the Dürer tradition sets in.

ii. The Great Multitude of chapter vii, adoring God and the Lamb. Here and elsewhere the presence of the ringed nimbus is to be noted.

iii. The Great Angel of chapter x, with his gold face. Seven faces on *r*. represent the Seven Thunders whose utterances John was forbidden to write.

iv. The Lion distributes the Vials to the Angels. I know no better reason for selecting the Lion than that he happens to be mentioned first among the Four Beasts. We find instances—not many—of the Eagle distributing the Vials, and a few of the Ox. The Man I have never found in this connexion.

Now, to speak in similar detail of the Second Family copies is a far more formidable task. I think I shall be well advised if I begin by introducing a member of it which is as early in date as any—contemporary, indeed, with the First Family—and represents a certain transition from the one group to the other: perhaps it would be more correct to say that it shows a stage at which the Second Family tradition has not been completely formed.

This book is the great Apocalypse of Trinity College, Cambridge, which has been reproduced in full for the Roxburghe Club. Unlike most, it is of a tall folio size, not a square book, and, in consequence, its pictures are not confined to any one part of the page, and vary in size. It is a quite magnificent work of art—I think, the finest of all Apocalypses—dating from not later than 1250, and undoubtedly English. Its text is in Anglo-French with the Berengaudus gloss. Like the First Family copies, it begins with scenes (8) from the Life of John. Like them (only more so!) it gives more scenes (22) at the end, adding to the First Family selection a picture of the murder of Domitian, which is found nowhere else, expanding the story of the sticks and stones turned to gold and jewels, and giving the whole story of the Young Robber, which occurs in but one other copy (Add. 35166). Other points of contact with the First Family are the blending of the Seven Churches with the Vision of Christ (no illustrations of the Letters being given). Also, the Rider on the Pale Horse has a bowl (not flaming): demons tread out the Vintage: the final picture is of John adoring Christ.

On the other hand, we note differences. The four angels found in Euphrates are, if not demons (as we shall sometimes find them) at least very sinister dark-faced beings. There are no pictures of Antichrist. The Beast crushes the hand of the Witness (this being the earliest occurrence): the Eagle, not the Lion, gives the Vials: there is no separate picture of Hell mouth. There is, besides, a scene, rather grotesque, which I have never found anywhere else. In chapter x John eats the little book given him by the angel, and, says the text, 'in my mouth it was sweet as honey, and when I had eaten it my belly was bitter'. The picture shows John in evident discomfort. These are important differences. It is also to be mentioned that Franciscan and Dominican friars are prominent in some of the pictures, as well as Benedictine monks. This should point to a date when the preaching orders were known in this country and had not yet embroiled themselves with the monks.

There is uncertainty, alas, as to the place of origin of this great book. I have favoured St. Albans, conscious as I am of the awkwardness of supposing that one and the same scriptorium could produce two different types of Apocalypse. But others have accepted the view, though some, for instance Mr. Cockerell, on whose opinion I lay great weight, disagree. You will ask if technically the pictures in the Trinity Apocalypse are allied to the St. Albans picture-books. They differ in important respects: for instance, the backgrounds here are fully coloured, and so are all draperies. This eliminates the ringed nimbus, for that is only usable on a plain background; yet I must note that the nimbuses here are very frequently edged with white dots, which are the equivalent of the rings.

Wherever the book was done, it is a highly important member of our series, the work of two extremely accomplished artists, and though in some respects—size, arrangement of pictures, and inclusion of certain subjects—it stands by itself, it has innumerable affinities with both the First and Second Families, and is not independent of —in fact, closely follows—the prevailing tradition.

[Examples shown:

1. The first page with scenes from the Life of John, from his preaching to his being brought before the Provost of Ephesus. The first artist of the book makes John beardless, and the second gives him a beard. The practice in regard of this detail seems to be capricious. Quite early and quite late books make him beardless: in the thirteenth-century copies there is perhaps a majority in favour of a beard.

2. *a.* John weeps because no one is found worthy to open the Book.

b. The Lamb takes the Book, and is adored by Angels, by the Elders, and by all Creation. This last touch is extremely uncommon.

3. By the second artist. The great Angel of chapter x, and the whole episode of the Little Book, with the rather grotesque scene which I have described.

4. *a.* The Throne in heaven and the Elders.

b. The Lamb on Mount Sion. The figure standing with his back turned occurs again in other treatments of this subject.

5. *a.* The First Judgement, presided over by Saints, not by God. This is correct according to the text.

b. The Siege of the Holy City and the binding of the Dragon.

6. The New Jerusalem, in quasi-ground-plan: by another artist. The central panel is gold, beautifully patterned. The arrangement may recall the corresponding picture in Mr. Thompson's Beatus MS. It is not very unfrequent.

7. From the second set of scenes of John's Life: unfinished, and without inscriptions. The subjects are

a. The repentance of the Robber Youth and perhaps his being set apart for the episcopate.

b. Christ (as it should be: the artist seems uncertain) and Apostles appearing to John to forewarn him of approaching death.

c. John addressing the people for the last time. On *r.* a grave is being dug for him at his command.]

The next step puts us at the head of a number of diverging paths. A method of exploring them must be chosen.

I will speak first of the half-page picture copies of the Second Family, then of those which contain a French version in prose or metre and have not the half-page system, mentioning in each case their allies: then of copies which are obviously nonconformist.

Of the half-page copies there is a small group which prefixes scenes of the Life of John to the text and adds a sequel at the end. I call this 'Life and Death of John'. One such is in the British Museum (Add. 35166), certainly an English book. It is the only one (as I have said) besides the great Trinity MS. which gives the story of the Young Robber.

Another is the Paris MS. B.N. lat. 688, which Delisle thought might be Spanish, and the ancestor of a fine fifteenth-century copy at the Escorial, of which something will be said later. Some specimens I have procured from it do not confirm this idea. The work is rough: the compositions agree most closely with those of a third, an English copy belonging to Mr. Dyson Perrins and recently reproduced in full by him. This Perrins book is defective at the end, but has the Life of John at the beginning, and its resemblance not only to Paris 688 but also to 35166 leads me to believe that it also had the Death of John.

At present I look upon Add. 35166 and *Perrins* as English examples, and on Paris 688 as a copy of an English example, and provisionally reckon them as adherents of the St. Albans group represented by the First Family copies.

[Examples from *Perrins*:

1. Not of common occurrence: the people rejoicing—dancing and feasting—at the death of the Two Witnesses.

2. The birds summoned to feast on the carcases of the kings and chieftains.]

These, then, are the books which have (or had) the Life *and Death* of John portrayed in them.

Then there are some which prefix scenes of the Life of John to the text, but have none at the end; and yet are complete. One such, at Trinity College, Cambridge (No. 213) is certainly English. It has Latin text and Berengaudus gloss. From certain pictures at the end which illustrate the life of Edward the Confessor, pretty exactly as we find them carved on the back of the altar screen in Westminster Abbey, I infer a Westminster connexion for this book: and, *à propos* of that, I remark that in the Westminster Chapter-house, where there was an Apocalypse painted on the walls, enough of the cycle is left to show that the Life of John began it, and there was no sequel of later scenes.

Another of the group is a French MS., with French text and gloss, of which the present whereabouts is unknown, since 1879, when it was sold by Schlesinger. And allied to the group is a pair of picture-books done for English nunneries, of which one is at Eton (177) and the other at Lambeth (434). These have a shortened text of the Book in French and no gloss. The Eton MS. seems to have some connexion with Worcester: at least, a series of typological pictures prefixed to the volume agrees closely with the series of wall-paintings which are recorded as having been in the Chapter-house at Worcester. These two books conform to the First Family tradition in some respects. The Rider on the Pale Horse has his bowl of fire: the Witnesses are slain with the sword: the Lion gives the Vials to the Angels: the last picture is of John adoring Christ. The New Jerusalem is shown in quasi-ground-plan, recalling the Trinity MS.

Very likely what I have here said of the Eton and Lambeth copies is true of the other MSS. I have mentioned, but my information is incomplete.

Next we have a group, still of half-page picture copies,

which have no scenes at all of St. John's life, but begin with the picture of him reclining on Patmos and addressed by an angel. Patmos is sometimes surrounded by other islands, and sometimes these have names, and sometimes not.

Members of this group are:

(**16**) A MS. formerly Mr. H. Y. Thompson's 55, now in private hands in Paris.

(**44**) The Lambeth MS. 209, already mentioned in another connexion. Both of these are English.

(**5**) A MS. at Cambrai, 482.

(**6**) One at Metz, de Salis Collection 38.

(**8**) One at the Seminary at Namur.

(**12**) Paris Bib. Nat. 14410, from the abbey of S. Victor.

(**13**) Brit. Mus. Add. 17333 with text in Latin and French, from the Chartreuse of Vaudieu between Liége and Aix. Artistically this is one of the best of the group.

(**15**) A MS. owned by a Dr. Rey, now in private hands in Paris.

These six are French books.

Of the Cambrai, Metz, probably Namur, and Add. 17333 we can say, thanks to Mr. Eric Millar's researches (*Bulletin S.F.R.M.* 1924) that they are copies of an archetype —doubtless English—which was like Lambeth 209. And the Lambeth book has a connexion with St. Augustine's, Canterbury. It also resembles with curious closeness the Thompson MS. There seems, indeed, to be absolute identity of text: the same errors appear in both. But Mr. Thompson's MS differs from it and from almost all others in having not only seventy-six pictures of the Apocalypse, but seventy-six of the interpretation thereof. To this point I shall have to return.

Taking some of the details which have been noted in other cases, I observe that these MSS. agree in giving the Rider on the Pale Horse a vessel of fire; making the Beast crush the hand of the Witness; showing devils in the Vintage scene, and the Lion distributing the Vials. They have also the large Hell mouth—sometimes with a butterfly beside it, which seems a curious adjunct. Somewhat similar is the introduction of an owl into the picture of the New Jerusalem. The last picture is of John adoring Christ.

I have ventured, on the strength of the Canterbury connexion of Lambeth 209, to label this group the Canterbury group.

Then we have a small subgroup consisting (at present) of three copies, all clearly English, viz.:

(**63**) Magdalene College Cambridge no. 5.
(**46**) Bodl. Canonici Bibl. 62.
(**86**) Bodl. Tanner 184.

The third and last is rather rougher and poorer in execution than the other two, which are both very good, and are remarkable for the fineness of the flourishing which surrounds the initials. Each has seventy-eight pictures and the agreement in composition is close. The Magdalene book has a rhyme about Crowland written in it, the Canonici to my eye resembles some Peterborough MSS.; the Tanner gives no clue to its provenance. These faint indications lead me, while attaching these books to the Canterbury rather than to the St. Albans group, to look to the Peterborough district as the place of origin. They agree in having the Berengaudus gloss in Latin, and in a peculiar arrangement of the writing on their first pages. The text of the page is continued into the inscription of the scroll held by St. John: the text ends 'in insula que appellatur' and the scroll goes on 'Pathmos propter uerbum dei', &c. Here the Rider on the Pale Horse has the bowl of fire, but is represented as Death. The Beast and Witnesses are as before: the devils are at the Vintage: the Lion gives the Vials. The Hell mouth picture is not in the same form as above, a demon being added who thrusts his colleagues into the Hell mouth: but the final picture is of John adoring Christ.

I have reserved till now the mention of another half-page picture copy which is a formidable candidate for the first place among these Apocalypses, viz., the Bodleian MS. Douce 180, which has been reproduced in full for the

Roxburghe Club by Mr. C. St. John Hornby. It consists of (*a*) a French prose version of the Apocalypse with the non-Berengaudus gloss and without pictures; (*b*) of a pictured Apocalypse in Latin with the Berengaudus gloss. The prefixed French version has in its initial figures of Edward I of England and his queen. The traces of a label on the damaged arms and the absence of a crown seem to show that it is earlier than 1272, when Edward succeeded. There is great similarity between the writing of the French text and that of the Latin. When we ask whether the work of either or both parts is English or French, disagreement arises. There is all the delicacy of the finest French hands in it. But the inscriptions on scrolls in the pictures are original, and are in Anglo-French, not French French. M. Meyer unhesitatingly classed it among English-written copies, and M. Delisle agreed. High authorities are unconvinced: the work is too fine to be English. Evidence of an external kind has been adduced: Mr. Cockerell, Mr. Millar, and others have pointed out the affinity in the drawing of faces and hands (this last a most remarkable feature) that subsists between the MS. and the lovely retable in Westminster Abbey. That there is community of school here—perhaps even of artist—is undeniable. Only, we are not sure whether the retable is English or French.

I am for England: the MS. shares some of the peculiarities of my Canterbury group, and to Canterbury, where French influence was very strong, I assign it until I am forced to relinquish that position.

Douce begins at once with John on Patmos: it gives names to the islands, being in these respects akin to the Canterbury group. It has a separate picture for each of the Seven Letters to the Churches; anomalous in this, anomalous also in giving the Rider on the Pale Horse a crossed nimbus, and making him like Christ. The death of the Witnesses, blended with the following scene, shows the Beast attacking the hand of the Witness. In the scene of the Lamb on Mount Sion some of the saints are represented as lambs (we shall find this again) and some as human beings. There are no devils in the scene of the Vintage. The Eagle, not the Lion, distributes the Vials. When the Sixth Vial is poured on Euphrates that the way of the Kings from the East may be prepared, we see the Kings: this is a rare phenomenon. Equally rare is a separate picture of the devil cast down into the earth (ch. xii) and another of the Scarlet Woman drunk. Unique as far as I know is an illustration of xxii. 15, 'Without are dogs', &c., combined with a picture of the Blessed washing their robes. The final scene is of John adoring Christ. In his choice of subjects and in a tendency to multiply his pictures, this artist stands by himself, as he assuredly does also in his power and his refinement. Many of his pictures are unfinished, and a considerable number in outline only. In these can most clearly be shown (in reproduction) his marvellous quality, since his admirable colouring cannot here be duly honoured.

The departures from the common path which I have mentioned are evidence of independence, of course: but since most of them have a parallel somewhere, I also conclude that the artist was so placed that he had access to several types of Apocalypses, and selected from them as seemed good to him.

[Six examples of his work were shown:

1. The Letter to Philadelphia. The illustrations of all the Letters are conceived on the same plan, and, beautiful as they are, there is no attempt to grapple with the contents of the Letters.

2. The Lamb on Mount Sion with lambs *and* saints about Him.

3. The Angel bidding John write Beati mortui.

4. The Sixth Vial and the Kings from the East.

5. The Scarlet Woman drunken with the blood of the saints: as I said, this is an infrequent picture.

6. Christ in glory: below His feet are souls washing their robes: on the *r.* dogs and men—sorcerers, idolaters, &c.—are going out, and an idol falls.]

Since these Lectures were composed and delivered, a book has been revealed which I cannot but believe to be another work of the artist of *Douce*. This is no. **50** on my list, the Paris MS. lat. 10474. Nothing in Delisle's brief decription of it suggested that it was particularly interesting: the first hint came from Miss O. E. Saunders's *English Illumination*, in which some examples from it are given as English work, and the resemblance with *Douce* is noted. The great kindness of Mr. C. H. St. John Hornby (who had *Douce* reproduced for the Roxburghe Club) has now procured me a complete set of photographs of the Paris MS., and it is imperative that some account of it should be given here. It came to Paris from the Jesuit College of Lyons at the Revolution. Earlier owners were a Pierre de Noalhes in the sixteenth century, a Villeneufve (cent. xvii), a Lenoir later. At the end is a poor fifteenth-century drawing of the Crucifixion, and a monogram of *IHC*, which might well be English.

The text occupying the lower half of the page, in double columns of nineteen lines, is in Latin with Berengaudus gloss. It shows such an agreement with that of *Douce* as to make it clear that both are copied from a single archetype.

Thus the two books agree in calling each section of the text an *Epistola*[1]: in displacing some pieces of gloss because of want of room on the proper page, and adding notes in identical terms to explain this: in omitting, by *homoeoteleuton*, exactly the same words in xvii. 15, 16.

It is equally plain that neither MS. is a copy of the other, for each contains portions of the gloss which are not in the other. The archetype therefore contained a more copious selection from the commentary of Berengaudus than does either of its descendants. But, it may be added, this selection was not intelligently made: the excerptor's aim was to give the whole text of the Apocalypse in sections, and to append to each section as much of the gloss as his page could hold. After copying so much of the beginning of each piece of commentary as he had room for, he breaks off,

[1] They do so in certain notes which explain displacements of the gloss. I suppose the writer hit upon *Epistola* as corresponding to *Evangelium*, in the sense of a liturgical Gospel.

disregarding sense, when he has filled his space. He rarely omits anything in the body of his extract. So his archetype will also have been a pictured MS.

The scribes of *Par* and *Douce* are not the same. In *Par* the text is written in one hand throughout: at first the gloss is written by that same hand; later it seems to have been added after the text was finished. In *Douce* text and gloss are throughout in one beautiful hand: that of the text larger than in *Par*, that of the gloss smaller. *Douce*, abhorring a vacuum, repeats bits of gloss to fill the page: *Par* does not.

In *Par* the spelling *ewangelium*, *ewangelista* occurs, which I believe to be an English—at least not a French—habit.

The pictures, half-page, are 90 in number. The first ten are fully coloured, nos. 11–42 have had the gold only inserted, the remainder are wholly in outline. Two leaves are gone; one had the Vision of Christ and Letter to Ephesus, the other (also, oddly enough, lost in *Douce*) had the Vision of Heaven (ch. iv) and Adoration of the Elders.

In *Douce* there are 97 pictures: 6 are missing. The excess is accounted for thus: in 8 cases *Douce* has 2 pictures where *Par* has one: in one case *Par* has 2 where *Douce* has one: and *Douce* adds two pictures at the end which *Par* has not.

Broadly the cycles agree. Both begin with John on Patmos, the islands being named: the Letters to the Churches are illustrated: there are separate pictures for the people rejoicing over the dead Witnesses, of the Dragon cast into the earth, of the Drunkenness of the Woman: the Eagle distributes the Vials: in the picture of the Lamb on Lion the saints are lambs. These are all marked features.

But, as one must expect when a really distinguished artist is in question, the agreement is not slavish: the differences are not few. In the very first picture the composition in *Par* is reversed in *Douce*: in the Letters *Par* gives no angels to the Churches: his Fourth Rider is not in the semblance of Christ: his angels in Euphrates are demons: he does not show us the Kings from the East: and so forth.

But the identity of the artist with the artist of *Douce* is to me apparent.

Par is a less finished production (I do not mean in regard of its colouring) than *Douce*: the script of the text is less fine and the whole lay-out of the book inferior. How it comes about that neither book has been completed we cannot expect to learn; perhaps we may be warranted in saying that it was this artist's habit to 'rough out' the whole work and finish it as he felt inclined. It is at least an additional mark of kinship between the books.

There is nothing in the history of *Par* and nothing that I can detect in its aspect to invalidate the thesis of an English origin; which may even be confirmed by such a detail as the spelling Ewangelium.

In some of the details wherein *Par* differs from *Douce* it agrees with other English copies, notably *Perrins*; and I am strengthened in my belief that it was produced at an important centre where more than one type of pictured Apocalypse are accessible.

In the Notes I give further details.

I have now dealt with all the half-page picture copies that are of any importance (some few having remained out of my reach). I subjoin to them one which is not widely known, that of Trinity College, Dublin (K. 4. 31). It can be placed in no other class, but it differs from the ordinary copies in having merely the Latin text without any gloss; and also in the form of its pictures, which are sexfoils set in square frames and with diapered grounds. There is a peculiar habit, too, of placing a large bust of Christ in a half-trefoil at the top of the picture. A leaf with two pictures is lost at the beginning, but an original numbering shows that no Life of John can have been prefixed. The whole number of pictures was seventy-five: seventy-three remain. Some directions for services, which, with an imperfect copy of the Meditations of St. Bernard, follow, indicate that the owner of the book was an ecclesiastic, and probably a monastic personage.

The Second Family tradition is followed pretty closely in the cycle, but there are deviations. The Rider on the Pale Horse has no bowl of fire. The Beast tramples on the Witnesses, but does not crush the hand of one. The Adoration of the Beast, and the Harpers, are unlike what I have seen elsewhere. The Vintage of the Earth is made into two pictures, in one of which is a large devil: the New Jerusalem also occupies two pages; the last picture is of John kneeling and an angel with a book.

[The examples shown:

1. The Adoration of the Beast. He is elevated on a pedestal on which he couches. The False Prophet is below on *l.* and on *r.* a purchaser of goods is pointing to the mark on his forehead to show that he is qualified to buy.

2. The Lamb is adored. Above Him are two harpers very curiously set *in* the woodwork of their harps. It is true that the Latin text has 'citharizantium *in* citharis suis' but I should have thought that that idiom was too familiar to mislead even a very simple-minded artist.

3, 4. The two pictures of the New Jerusalem. The angel and John in the first, the city in the second, with three domes, and an angel in every gate.

In the first picture the large bust of Christ appears.]

III

The distinguishing mark of all the books we have been considering so far is that they are *picture-books*—the pictures being on the whole the first consideration. Indeed, in the Douce book the text is so carelessly (though beautifully) written as sometimes to make nonsense. It should be added, as evidence that the text was a subsidiary affair, that a great many of the half-page picture copies omit all but the addresses of the Seven Letters and also a great part of the seventeenth and eighteenth chapters, relating to Babylon, and portions of the two last chapters besides; thus discarding all the matter that did not appear in the pictures. The First Family books, we have seen, have only a minimum of text, written on the pictures. In the Paris book 403 and the Trinity book the text is much more important: yet broadly speaking one may claim that these are picture-books. A number of them have vernacular texts. This means that they were designed for the use of people who did not read much, and who preferred French to Latin. In two cases we are sure that the users were nuns; in another (Douce) it was a king or queen. The Trinity book was once in royal hands: it has a binding by Berthelet of *c.* 1550–60 with the crown and royal arms; and I believe it was made for Henry III's queen, Eleanor of Provence. The Paris book has a late and absurd inscription to say that it was done for Charlemagne. The Lambeth MS. belonged, it seems, to a Lady de Quincy. In short, we may say with some confidence that all the best copies were made for the use of lay persons of quality.

The next group we have to examine are not so much picture-books as illustrated books, the pictures being on the whole subsidiary to the text. They are usually set in any convenient place on the page, and their shapes and sizes vary. The groups in question include the copies which have a French metrical version and those with a French prose version. The metrical version M. Paul Meyer has printed in *Romania*, xxv. According to him it was made in England, and has little literary value. Of this group there seem to be nine copies, divisible into families (details of which are not important at the moment) and all of English execution: none is of fine artistic quality. The pictures represent the Second Family tradition, but have some curious variants, not all found in all copies. Thus the four angels in Euphrates are demons. When the Witnesses are slain, it is done by Antichrist crowned and winged, with a sword. A separate picture shows people rejoicing over them (so also in the Douce and Perrins copies). The Beast of ch. xiii is not a quadruped but a biped with human body and seven heads. The Lamb on Sion has other lambs about Him. Lastly, in ch. xx, the Holy City is besieged by dog-headed men in one copy at least. This is a significant detail, reminiscent of Eastern tradition, as we shall see anon.

As to the owners of these copies: one, at Corpus Christi College, Cambridge, was given by a Countess of Huntingdon to St. Augustine's, Canterbury: another, at the Fitzwilliam Museum, belonged to a nunnery at Nuneaton.

We pass to the French *prose* version copies: quite twelve of these are of English make, and few of first-class execution. The best no doubt is that in the British Museum, 19. B. xv, with its beautiful white figures on grounds of blue or red, which has been made known by several publications of single pages. One of the artists of it was also employed on Queen Mary's Psalter (2. B. vii).

Now these books also, so far as I have examined them, agree in certain peculiarities, though not all of them in all. Their first picture is usually one of John addressing a seated group of people. In ch. iv he climbs a ladder to the door opened in Heaven. At the Vintage of the Earth, no devils are present: sometimes men tread the grapes instead. The last picture, again, is of John addressing a group of people.

Locally, I associate this group with eastern England. The bosses in the cloisters of Norwich Cathedral are copied from a MS. of this type. One of the British Museum examples (15. D. ii) belonged to a Lincolnshire nunnery. These are meagre indications, but not without importance.

Of the copies of French make I have really nothing to say. I have seen hardly any of them, but, judging from Delisle's descriptions, there are none of outstanding merit.

Now I turn to what I must call the interpretative group. Side by side with the illustrations of the text of the Apocalypse, some few books give us pictures setting forth the spiritual or the historical meaning of the Book. I will enumerate the members of this small and not homogeneous class. They are:

16. A MS. formerly Mr. H. Y. Thompson's No. 55, already mentioned. In its Apocalypse-pictures and its text it is closely akin to Lambeth 209, and thus connected with the Canterbury group. Left unfinished by its English producer, it was exported to Italy, and the colouring at least completed there.

73. The Apocalypse in the *Bible moralisée*, which Bible was an enormous undertaking due, I believe, to S. Louis. The whole Bible is illustrated in medallion-pictures, and its meaning elucidated in a parallel set of medallions. The finest and oldest copy is (most of it) at Toledo. The whole work has been reproduced by the Comte de Laborde.

These two books are of the thirteenth century.

74. The marginal illustrations in the Bedford Hours include a full treatment of the Apocalypse. This book was done for John Duke of Bedford as Regent of France about 1420: it is a Paris work. It is in the British Museum, Add. 18850.

85. A large German fourteenth-century altar-piece in the Victoria and Albert Museum, perhaps by a Hamburg master.

Lastly there is the Commentary of Alexander on the Apocalypse.

The last three must be considered together.

The Thompson MS., we have seen, is a Second Family copy. Its interpretations include some few Biblical parallels; e.g. the Great Angel of ch. x is Christ coming into the world, and is illustrated by the Massacre of the Innocents and Flight into Egypt: but there is no attempt to explain the Apocalypse in terms of the history of the Church or of the world, though Franciscan friars are often introduced to typify the preachers of the last times. Similarly the *Bible moralisée* is here based on a Second Family MS., though the number of subjects ordinarily found in such a MS. is just doubled; we have 156 instead of seventy-eight. The familiar scenes of the Beast crushing the hand of the Witness, and the Lion giving the Vials, are here. The interpretation is in the main spiritual; but it is not the same as that of the Thompson MS.

The case of the Bedford Hours, the German altar-piece,

and Alexander's Commentary, is different. The last named must rank as the progenitor of the other two. The Commentary of Alexander the Minorite, or Alexander Laicus, as he is variously called, is a book not perfectly known and never printed in full. The best accessible account of it is by Mr. J. P. Gilson in *Collectanea Franciscana* (ii. 20). The author, he shows, was a Saxon, probably connected with the diocese of Bremen, and acquainted with the chronicler Albert of Stade: he borrows copiously from the *Annales Stadenses*. He wrote in 1242–3, and he interprets the Apocalypse in terms of the history of the Christian church down to his own time; so that the New Jerusalem stands for the Franciscan Order, of which he was a member.

There are not many copies of his book: the best is undoubtedly that in the University Library at Cambridge (Mm. 5. 31), which, though gravely mutilated, has a far fuller text, and a richer series of pictures, than any other. There are three MSS. of an abridged text: one in the Chapter Library at Prague, published in lithography in 1873; one at Breslau described by Prausnitz in the *Zentralblatt für Bibliothekswissenschaft*, 1921; one at Dresden (A. 117), fully described by Bruck in his *Malereien d. Hdss. d. königr. Sächsens* but without knowledge of the other copies. All are illustrated. The pictures set forth text and meaning together. Each of the Seven Churches, for example, has its historic first bishop beside it, Polycarp for Smyrna, Melito for Sardis, &c. The Third Rider, with the balances, is Titus, and in his balances we see the Jews whom he sold at thirty for a penny. The Trumpets herald the rise of great heretics, as Macedonius or Pelagius. The last of the Beasts is Sultan Saladin. All these personages are of course indicated by inscriptions.

From this book, directly or indirectly, are derived the interpretations in the Bedford Hours and on the German altar-piece. In the Bedford Hours there are 152 pairs of marginal medallions of the Apocalypse and its meaning, just about as many as in the *Bible moralisée*, but quite differently arranged. For instance, a pair of medallions is devoted to each of the Twelve Tribes, of whom 12,000 are sealed. The German altar-piece is incomplete: in forty-five scenes it gets as far as the Seventh Vial (ch. xvi). Its lengthy inscriptions, many of them defective, give the same historical interpretation as Alexander, and I am tempted to think that Alexander may have been the *immediate* authority, for I see a peculiarity common to both which does not depend on the commentary. It is that the Ox is distributing the Vials to the Angels. This is not without a parallel, but is rare. In the other case I think (in view of the rarity of MSS. of Alexander) that the immediate source must have been the fourteenth-century commentary of Nicholas de Lyra, who follows Alexander, and whose book was to be had everywhere.

The exigencies of Alexander's interpretation take him so far off the beaten track that many of his pictures have little resemblance to the traditional ones. On the tradition, however, they are based, and moreover, so far as I can see, on the Second Family cycle.

Before leaving the thirteenth and fourteenth centuries, outside which we have hardly trespassed at all, let something be said of the use of the Apocalypse in works of art that are not books, particularly sculpture, wall-painting, tapestry, and glass. There is not a great deal.

The southern side-portal of the west front of Rheims cathedral has sculptures of the Apocalypse: some sixty groups in the voussures of the arch illustrate practically the whole Book; a more conventional Last Judgement fills the gable: and round the corner on the south side are the Life of John and his death, showing that the model was a MS., if not of the First Family, then of the group which contains the whole story.

I have mentioned the series of bosses in the cloisters at Norwich as representing a MS. of the French prose version type. This cycle occupies the south and west walks of the cloister, and was put up in the late fourteenth and early fifteenth century: I have described it fully in a publication of the Norfolk and Norwich Archaeological Society. It is not complete, but contains about ninety groups, by no means easy to decipher.

It may be worth while to repeat here the observation that the great compositions of the Last Judgement which fill so many of the portal-tympana in France and elsewhere are not dependent on the Apocalypse for their main features.

In wall-painting the examples known to me are not many. Two are Italian, and from what I can learn of them they seem to be modelled on the Anglo-French cycle. One is of the late thirteenth century in the Upper Church at Assisi, by Cimabue. The Seals, the Angels holding the Winds, the Fall of Babylon at least are distinguishable among much that has perished. More complete and including about thirty subjects is a cycle ascribed to Giusto Menabuoi which forms part of the copious fresco decoration of the Baptistery at Padua. In this case the dependence on a model of the Anglo-French type is not doubtful.

In France I can only point to some paintings (much restored and of which I could make little) on the vaulting of the church of S. Macaire in Gironde, and to a figure of one of the Riders on the crypt roof at Auxerre Cathedral. There must surely be more than these, but I have failed to find more. In England we have the beginning and other fragments of a long series in the Westminster Chapter-house, already mentioned: it is of the end of the fourteenth century, and about twenty-five subjects out of perhaps over 100 arc recognizable. There is also mention in an eighteenth-century source of a set of wall-paintings in Beachley church, Gloucestershire, which must long have perished.

Tapestry has one very important monument to show in the almost complete set of hangings belonging to the cathedral of Angers. These were begun at the order of Louis, Duke of Anjou, in 1377 or so by Nicolas Bataille of Paris, and the cartoons were drawn by Jean or Hennequin de Bruges, King's painter. It has been confidently said that the designs were modelled on the Paris MS. fr. 403. A note in the oldest inventory of the Louvre Library says, indeed, that this MS. was lent by the King to M. d'Anjou 'pour faire faire son beau tapis'. But if lent, it was not found suitable, and not used. M. Delisle has shown beyond a doubt that the tapestry is copied from a more ordinary Second Family MS. There were seven pieces in the set, containing in all eighty-four scenes and six large figures under canopies. Thirteen scenes are now lost and four more are incomplete. The series begins with John and the Seven Churches. The Rider on the Pale Horse is represented as Death, with a sword, not a bowl of fire. The Beast crushes the hand of one of the Witnesses. There is a devil in the Vintage scene: the Lion gives the Vials. The kings from the East are shewn. The two last panels are gone. There is little that can serve to fix the exact group to which the MS. model belonged, but that it was a half-page picture copy is pretty evident.

I am rather surprised to find so little use of the Apocalypse in glass as I do. For instance, at Chartres there is only the southern rose, which gives the Majesty with the Four Beasts and the Elders. Such roses occur elsewhere with fair frequency, but, like the mosaics of earlier times, show only a single scene, not a cycle. Bourges has a window called of the Apocalypse, but in fact the Vision of Christ among the candlesticks is the only picture taken from the Book: the rest is symbol. Auxerre once had an Apocalypse in glass; a few medallions remain, enough to show that the Life and Death of John found a place in it. These works are of the thirteenth century.

In England we have one fine monument in the eighty-one panels of the lower part of the great east window of York Minster, dating from the earliest years of the fifteenth century. I have had the advantage of using a set of careful drawings of these, which show that scenes from the Life of John were prefixed, but there were none at the end.

The Lion gives the Vials: the Kings of the East appear at the Sixth Vial. By the help of the drawings I was able to settle the right order of the panels, in which there is at present chaos in certain parts of the window. The corrected order will be found in Mr. Harrison's recent book on the York glass.

In Blomefield's *Norfolk* there is record of Apocalypse windows at Snetterton, and of a window of Antichrist at Griston. Nothing survives at either place.

I have not found any other Apocalypse windows anterior to the sixteenth century, and all those of the sixteenth century that I have seen draw their inspiration from Dürer's woodcuts.

Have I now made good my assertion that the Second Period of Apocalypse illustration is characterized by uniformity, by a settled tradition? I believe I have so far as the English and French MSS. and monuments are concerned. But there are, not unnaturally, certain outliers, as to whose relation to the main line of tradition I am uncertain.

For instance, Venturi in his fifth volume (fig. 803, &c.) gives some examples of Apocalypse illustrations from an Italian Bible, and d'Agincourt some others from a New Testament of the thirteenth century (Vat. Lat. 39) which suggest that Italy was not wholly dominated by the Anglo-French cycle. But a fourteenth-century Apocalypse at Florence with Italian text and full-page pictures of poor quality, does seem, if I may judge from incomplete information, to depend on the familiar tradition.

Similarly, Germany seems to stand aloof. German Apocalypses are not common, but three books, one a fragment, are known to me which have a cycle of full-page compositions. One has been reproduced in full by H. v. d. Gabelentz: it is at Weimar, of the fourteenth century, appended to a *Biblia Pauperum*. The number of pictures is twenty-five, and they do not show marked resemblance to those with which we are familiar. Another in the British

Museum (Add. 15243) is clearly not independent of the Weimar MS., and a fragment at Nuremberg is, equally clearly, copied from Weimar. A Hamburg MS. of Cent. xiv is apparently more normal, but not remarkable for beauty. Whatever the relationships, the German cycle is not important: unless indeed it chances to have been the progenitor, through the medium of illustrated Bibles, of the compressed cycle which Dürer embodied in his woodcuts.

We now return for a short time to the Anglo-French cycle and witness its dying out. In the course of the fifteenth century very few pictured Apocalypses were produced, apart from the Block-books. A handsome MS. in the Fitzwilliam Museum, the Hours of Isabel of Brittany (*c.* 1430), has, like the Bedford Hours, marginal illustrations, numbering 139, of the Apocalypse. It is a very normal series, though by various devices it is spun out to an unwonted length. One such device is to represent the sending and the delivery of each of the Seven Letters, so as to make fourteen precisely similar scenes: but the matter of the Letters is not hinted at. A Second Family copy has been the source drawn upon.

Among fifteenth-century Apocalypses it seems probable that one at the Escorial, executed for the House of Savoy, and alluded to above, must rank as the best. It contains work of two periods; the earlier portion has pictures by Jean Bapteur, and borders by Perronnet Lamy (done in 1428–35), the later portion is by Jean Colombe of Bruges (1482). It is a half-page copy, with Latin text and Berengaudus gloss, and pictures of the Life and Death of John. The few accessible reproductions of pages from it show that the work of both the illustrators is extremely fine, and that a Second Family copy was their model. A few more particulars are given in the Notes.

There is a remarkable series of compositions in a Low Country MS. (Paris B.N. néerlandais 3). This has twenty-three full-page pictures, one for the Life of John, the rest for the twenty-two chapters of the Book. Each of these contains the matter of several pictures of the ordinary cycle. Interesting features are these: the attempt to illustrate the contents of the Seven Letters: the representation of the Rider on the Pale Horse as Death: a series of groups, to me obscure, which accompany the picture of the Great Multitude: a borrowing from the First Family of the story of Antichrist in ch. xi. There is no demon at the Vintage. The Lion distributes the Vials. Features of the conventional Last Judgement are introduced at ch. xx. The colouring of these pictures is said to be very fine. They are evidently the work of two, and I think only two, artists. A description of the whole series will be found in the Notes.

In the Huth Collection was an unusual copy (lot 232 in the Sale of Nov. 1911) of which I do not know the present whereabouts. It has seventy-eight pictures in very fine French-Flemish style of the second half of the fifteenth century. Once owned by Mr. Johnson of the Oxford Observatory, it finds a mention in Waagen's *Treasures of Art* (iii. 112). Its text is in French with a long gloss. The heraldry shows that it was written for Margaret of York, Edward IV's sister, who married Charles the Bold in 1468. The pages reproduced in the sale catalogue show pictures at the top of the bordered page and text in *lettre bâtarde* written in double columns below. The subjects given are St. John and St. Paul (illustrating the Prologue), the Great Angel of ch. x, and St. John adoring the Angel in ch. xxii. As the MS. has 124 leaves, many pages must be without pictures. The evidence I have suggests that the old cycle was used, but very freely adapted.

The standard tradition does just trespass into the sixteenth century. For completeness' sake I mention a MS. in the Hunterian Collection at Glasgow, done, as the heraldry shows, for a member of the family of Poitiers. It must be, I think, the latest of all the half-page picture copies. It is imperfect, containing only the first fourteen chapters, and forty-eight pictures, but we can cheerfully dispense with the rest. The work is quite careful, but nowhere pleasing. The pictures are under architectural canopies, with angels holding shields. The text is in Latin and French.

Of the Block-books perhaps enough has been said to place them correctly. They are indubitably based on a First Family MS., no doubt one of the Low Country copies of an English archetype, with inscriptions on the pictures.

So ends a very long disquisition on the Second Period.

Before I embark on my far briefer treatment of the Third Period, I must divert to another region, and speak of the Apocalypse as treated in Eastern Christendom. I have done what I could at various times to ascertain whether there does indeed exist any ancient set of wall-paintings of the Apocalypse in Greek churches. Didron mentions some at Xeropotamou on Athos as following closely the directions in the Painter's Guide. Brockhaus (*Kunst d. Athosklostern*) ignores these and says there are no old Apocalypse paintings on Athos at all: some at Xenophontos may be of the sixteenth or seventeenth century. The Painter's Guide, which goes under the name of Dionysios Panselinos, is a very late production as we have it, but might embody in the relevant part of it, as it does in others, a fairly old tradition. It prescribes a cycle of twenty-four scenes, covering the whole field of the Apocalypse.

We saw above that traces of one or two Greek illustrations of our Book are in Herrade's twelfth-century *Hortus deliciarum*. But I have hitherto failed to find any indication that the Apocalypse as a separate book with pictures existed in Greek lands. Not even in the form of marginal illustrations of a New Testament. There was, however, a great output of illustrated Apocalypses in and after the sixteenth century in Russia. A large number of these were reproduced in 1884 by Busslaieff. In each case the number of pictures runs to about sixty or seventy. The books are late enough in date to have been obviously influenced by Dürer's woodcuts, but they also retain some features that must be Eastern. They usually have a picture of the Bride, the Lamb's wife, which is meant as a contrast to the figure of the Scarlet Woman. In their pictures of the Judgement they introduce (what we have seen in Herrade) beasts, birds, and fish giving up the portions of bodies they have devoured. And, in the siege of the Holy City, the assailants, Gog and Magog, are dog-headed. I have noted the occurrence of this in at least one Western MS., of the French metrical version group. It was quite possibly suggested by the Apocalypse attributed to St. Methodius, a writing which had a great vogue all over Europe in the Middle Ages.

More than this I do not know of the Apocalypse in eastern Europe: but I am persuaded that more is to be known.

Turning now to the Third Period, I observe that there is more than one way in which its Apocalypse illustrations are marked off from those of the Second.

In the first place, the cycle is very much compressed. The illustrated Bibles have not much more than twenty pictures of the Book. Dürer's woodcuts number fourteen, *plus* one of St. John in the cauldron of oil. Duvet gives twenty-four plates. We are reminded of the twenty-five pictures in the Weimar MS. and the twenty-three in the Flemish one at Paris.

Then, whereas the artists and expositors of the thirteenth century (with the exception of Brother Alexander) did not see in every detail of the Book a foreshadowing of definite events in history, there was a growing tendency to do so as the period of the Reformation drew nigh. To us nothing is more familiar than the view that Rome, the Papacy, is the Scarlet Woman, or Babylon. Need I say that this was not the idea of the thirteenth-century illustrator? But already in the Wittenberg Bible of 1522 the Scarlet Woman wears the triple crown. In this kind of way the controversies of the time are reflected in the illustration of the Book.

But, to consider the development. I believe that the *Bible Historiale* had a part to play in it. This book is a French version of the *Historia Scholastica* of Peter Comestor, with additions which include the Epistles and the Apocalypse. Not a few copies of it, while allotting as a rule only one picture to each Book (Genesis being an exception), give perhaps a dozen to the Apocalypse. When printed Bibles with woodcuts began to be issued, this same practice was followed in them. A Cologne Bible of 1480 and a Nuremberg Bible of Koberger's of 1483 modelled thereon have a series of this kind. Holbein's well-known Bible cuts have a similar origin. These Bibles were evidently familiar to Dürer when in 1498 he issued his set of woodcuts. One trait alone is enough to prove this: the representation of the Great Angel of ch. x with his legs 'like pillars of brass'. The artist of the woodcut Bible, unhappily inspired, gives these legs the appearance of large drain pipes with feet at the bottom. Dürer copies them, but omits the feet.

As to his cycle: After the picture of St. John in the cauldron, he begins with (1) the Vision of Christ among the candlesticks and passes to (2) the Majesty and the Lamb taking the sealed Book; (3) the Four Riders are the next, a famous composition, then (4) the Fifth and Sixth Seals; (5) the Angels of ch. vii, not holding the Four Winds as is usual, but threatening them with weapons, and the sealing of God's servants, follow; (6, 7, 8) the Great Multitude and the Trumpets occupy three more plates (but 8 is sometimes placed after 12); (9) the Great Angel comes next. The Witnesses are omitted; (10) The Woman clothed with the Sun and (11) the fight with the Dragon are the next two, and after that the story is very much compressed; (12) the Beast, False Prophet, and Harvest of the Earth are in one composition; (13) the Scarlet Woman and her fall in another; (14) the binding of the Dragon and the New Jerusalem make up the last. Thus chapters i–xii occupy eleven cuts: chapters xiii–xxii only three.

The Wittenberg Bible of 1522 already mentioned is one

of the first works in which Dürer is copied, in Germany: but here he is slightly expanded. Two separate cuts are made for the Fifth and Sixth Seals. A fresh design, of the Witnesses, is added. The Harvest and Vintage of the Earth are more fully illustrated, and the binding of the Dragon and the New Jerusalem are separated. This Bible proved a potent instrument for disseminating the conceptions of Dürer. It seems to have been the immediate model for the sets of cuts done in 1523 by Burgkmair, Schaüffelein, and Holbein, as also for those by Beham. Variations are introduced, of course, but, as M. Mâle says, the canon is now fixed. No one strikes out a really new line. In France, imitation of Dürer appears, I gather, earlier than in Germany. Hardouyn gives reduced forms of the cuts in the borders of a Book of Hours of 1507. The Wittenberg Bible also is copied in French Bibles.

But France has a really important descendant of Dürer to show in the twenty-four plates issued in 1561 by Jean Duvet. This artist, who did not please earlier critics, seems now to be coming into his own. An article by Mr. A. E. Popham of the British Museum is the most recent guide to knowledge about his life and work. 'The striking thing about his work is its unlikeness to that of his contemporaries, and its complete aloofness and independence. The spirit of it goes back to an age of simple and fervid religious belief, to the age of Giotto, and looks forward to a single personality, that of William Blake.' Such is Mr. Popham's general estimate: I quote him again in saying that technically Duvet's style of engraving is clearly founded on that of Marcantonio in his first Roman period.

He appears to have been working on his Apocalypse from 1546, by order of Francis I and Henry II. The first plate is dated 1555 when he was seventy, and the whole was only issued in 1561.

The set of twenty-four plates begins with one of Duvet himself, garbed as an antique or apostolic personage, studying the Apocalypse, by the side of a water over which the

Three Fates are being wafted towards him in a boat, implying, I suppose, that the end of his life is near. It proceeds with the vision of Christ among the candlesticks, the composition of which is Dürer's.

[Other examples of Dürer's and Duvet's work selected for exhibition were:

a. The Four Riders; Dürer's well-known cut, and Duvet's plate which is founded on it. As in his other borrowings, the scene is far more crowded, by the addition of many supplementary figures. This adds greatly to the movement, and helps to impart a right Apocalyptic atmosphere.

b. Duvet's plate of the Fifth Seal and of the Fifth Trumpet. Here we have the Souls under the Altar, and also the Star falling, and a devil (who should be an angel) opening Hell, and men perishing before the attacks of the Locusts. The picture is taken, as the label says, from the sixth and ninth chapters. The seventh and eighth are illustrated in the next plates.

c. Dürer's and Duvet's Great Angel of ch. x. Duvet keeps the unfortunate columnar legs, but has, I think, improved upon the original.

d. Dürer and Duvet. The Woman and the Dragon, where Duvet has kept very close to Dürer throughout.

e. Dürer and Duvet. The binding of the Dragon. Here Duvet has duplicated the motif of binding, showing Satan, as well as the Dragon, being bound. Though he has kept some of Dürer's landscapes he has preferred to make the New Jerusalem a separate plate, so that here his cities and towers have little meaning.]

His last three plates are devoted to the New Jerusalem, the River of Life, and John on Patmos.

I have said that Dürer's influence is paramount in the books and plates produced after his time. It is also paramount in other departments of art. I know of but one set of tapestries which is important to us. It is that at Madrid. Designed by some one of the school of Van Orley and bearing the mark of Pannemaker, these tapestries show coincidences with Dürer, as in the columnar legs of the Angel, but also reversion to the elder tradition, since the angels who restrain the winds are not threatening them with weapons

(Dürer's own idea) but stopping the mouths of human faces which they hold.

In sculpture I have noticed but little. One of the beautiful bishops' tombs in Limoges Cathedral, that of Jean de Langeac, of 1544, has a series of reliefs from the Apocalypse, modelled on Dürer.

As for painted glass, all the examples that I know of Apocalypse windows of this period are French. At S. Florentin in Yonne, at S. Martin des Vignes and S. Nizier at Troyes, at Granville and Chavanges in Aube and La Fertè Milon in Aisne (these three known to me through M. Mâle) are such windows, and in all of them, but perhaps most glaringly at S. Martin des Vignes, Dürer is copied or adapted. Noticeably all these places are within the sphere of influence of the glass painters of Troyes. At S. Jacques at Lisieux are remains of a series which seems to have filled twelve windows, of the early sixteenth century. One only is complete, and illustrates the Scarlet Woman and the armies of heaven. Further, in the chapel at Vincennes is a most remarkable set of Apocalypse windows, attributed by unconfirmed tradition to Jean Cousin, which were completed about 1558. Each window is occupied by a single scene. These (which I regret to say I have never seen) are characterized by M. Mâle as 'une des grandes choses du XVIe siècle'. They are, he says, a sort of translation of Dürer's Apocalypse into the language of the Italian Renaissance. Their designer appears to have had access to Dürer's engravings, but has also used some Bible dependent on the Wittenberg Bible of 1522; and M. Mâle sees a connexion, which he does not undertake to explain decisively, between the windows and the *Figures du Nouveau Testament* engraved by Petit Bernard and published at Lyons in 1553.

I have now reached a point at which I think it legitimate to break off my survey. The Apocalypse illustrations of succeeding times, where they are not adaptations of Dürer, are as sporadic and tentative as those of the First Period, and my researches among them have been equally sporadic. Dutch and German and English illustrated Bibles supply the greater part of the material that I have seen. Here and there a painter has covered wall or canvas, but his efforts are rarely remembered. Perhaps a word is due to John Martin of the early nineteenth century. His compositions have a note of their own: wide landscapes, crowds of small figures fleeing in panic, rocks falling, endless colonnades stretching upward to incredible heights, dark skies whence a flash of lightning invariably breaks forth. These impress at least the childish imagination, and I for one cannot deny them a certain poetic quality. It is the pitiless repetition that in the end makes them so cheap. That I should drag on the review through the Doré Bible, Cassell's Family Bible, &c., &c., down to the woodcuts of A. F. Cosyns, issued with Couchoud's French version of the Book in 1922 (these being the latest illustrations of the Apocalypse which I chance to have seen) is probably more than you expect, certainly more than I am in a position to do. So here the list of testimonies shall be definitely closed.

I did not expect to be, and I do not now find that I am, able to draw any broad conclusions affecting either art or literature from the study of this particular piece of history. My subject has been the appeal of the Apocalypse to the eye: to follow this up by investigating the influence of the Book upon the arts that appeal to the ear, more particularly the art of verse, would need quite other qualifications than I can bring to bear. In all the monuments we have been studying, the appeal is made to the eye, and in the majority of cases I suspect that a precise meaning was not asked for. If it was asked for, the interpretation of the Book which any or all of the glosses offered was not very helpful; if one excepts the historical exposition of Alexander and his group, it must be confessed that there was little actuality in them. They make a dismal contrast to the fervid visions of the seer himself. What remained in the mind of him or her who pored over the pictured Apocalypses was the panorama of tremendous signs in the heavens, heavens which opened ever and anon to show a supreme Throne and venerable shapes around it; of monstrous forms of evil looming up to dominate a frightened world; of colossal cavalcades advancing to destroy them; of the blare of trumpets, the voice of thunderings, the ringing of harps; and of one great final convulsion and purging of all things, out of which rises the Golden City, watered by the shining river, shaded by the Trees of Life, illumined—most wonderful—by a Lamb as it had been slain. And perhaps this was enough.

NOTES

LECTURE I

PAGE 31. The mosaic in S. Pudenziana, Rome, is figured in many text-books, e.g. V. Schultze, *Archäol. d. Christl. Kunst*, p. 230. That of SS. Cosma e Damiano, ibid., p. 238.

PAGE 32. Prudentius, *Dittochaeum*, xlix.

Apocalypsis Iohannis

Bis duodena senum sedes, pateris citharisque
Totque coronarum fulgens insignibus, Agnum
Caede cruentatum laudat: qui euoluere librum
Et septem potuit signacula pandere solus.

PAGE 32. Leo I's mosaic and Sergius's restoration of it are discussed, and the drawing in the Eton MS. figured, in *Röm. quartalschr. f. Alterthumskunde*, 1895, by H. Grisar. *Die alte Peterskirche zu Rom.* (pp. 227–98).

PAGE 33. The authority for Galla Placidia's apocalypse-pictures at Ravenna is Hieron. Rubeus *Hist. Ravennatum*, ii. (sub anno 433) ap. *Thes. Ital. Antiq.* vii. pt. i, col. 98.

'Videbatur autem in maiestate deus libellum Ioanni Euangelistae porrigens, cui erat subscriptum: Sanctus Ioannes Euangelista. Hinc atque inde mare vitreum in quo duae naves turbulenter tempestate et ventorum impetu agitatae; in altera diuus Ioannes Placidiae opem ferens aderat, septemque candelabra et nonnulla praeterea ex iis quae in Apocalypsi describuntur mysteria.' There follows an enumeration of the effigies of the imperial family, and a notice of a Majesty and other figures in the central cupola.

PAGE 33. Bede, Vitae Abbatum 5:

imagines evangelicae historiae quibus australem ecclesiae parietem decoraret; imagines visionum Apocalypsis beati Iohannis quibus septemtrionalem aeque parietem ornaret.

PAGE 34. The Trèves MS. Th. Frimmel, *Die Apokalypse in den Bilderhandschriften des Mittelalters*, 1885, gives a list and partial description of the pictures, and I a briefer one in the Trinity Apocalypse. This may be amplified here and a note of the corresponding Cambrai pictures given. Fascimiles of some pages are in K. Schellenberg, *Dürer's Apokalypse* (Monogr. z. Deutschen Kunst, iii), Munich, 1923: as noted below.

The colouring is simple: red-brown and yellow predominate. Frimmel seems to think that the grounds of the pictures were originally coloured. There is no gold or silver. The book belonged in the xi–xii cent. to the church of St. Eucharius at Trèves.

The text is in half uncial, extensively corrected in Cent. xii. It needs further examination.

1. f. 1 *b*. Rev. I. 1. The Angel and John. Under a triangular-headed portico, with two birds perched on the outer angles and a cross on the gable. John, beardless, on *r*. holds a roll. The hand of the angel on *l*. is extended towards him. Schellenberg, pl. 1.

In Cambrai (C) a round-headed arch is inserted and a tree is between the figures.

2. f. 2 *b*. Rev. I. 11. John and the Seven Churches. He stands on *l*. with roll. The churches are arranged in three rows, the lowest containing 3 buildings. One has 3 domes, another a single dome.

C. vacat.

3. f. 3 *b*. Rev. I. 7. Behold, he cometh with clouds.

Christ on *l*. half-length, holding a cross: He is beardless and cross-nimbed. Below, five people look up. Clouds above. On *r*. Angel with trumpet. John seated below with roll. A building with central dome, and water and fishes in front.

C. vacat.

4. f. 4 *b*. I. 12–18. The Vision of Christ.

In two tiers: above on *l*. four red candlesticks, on *r*. three. In *c*. Christ full length; an elliptical sword-blade proceeds from His mouth. He holds a brown and white cross and lays a hand on the head of John.

Below: John on Patmos. Water and fishes on *l*. John in *c*. A building on *r*.

C. vacat.

5. f. 5 *b*. I. 19, 20. The commission to write to the Churches.

On *l*. above, Christ half length with cross: below, John sits writing and looking up. In *c*. the Churches disposed as before. Each has its angel standing on *l*. near its doors. C. vacat.

6. f. 6 *b*. II. 1. Letter to Ephesus.

On *l*. above, Christ half-length. John stands: on *l*. of him are three trees, two with grapes: on *r*. another.

Below are four springs of water gushing from holes into water below.

'I will give him to eat of the tree of life.'

C. 2 arranges the trees differently.

7. f. 7 *b*. II. 8. Letter to Smyrna.

On *l*. above, Divine Hand out of cloud. John below. Angel and Church on *r*. Below, five people chained by the hands, the chain held by a devil, horned (damaged), seated in the doorway of a building.

'The devil shall cast some of you into prison.'

C. vacat.

8. f. 9 *b*. II. 12. Letter to Pergamos.

Above *l*. Christ, with extended hand. John on *r*.

Below, *l*, Angel and Church with campanile and portico with five Corinthian columns. Schellenberg, pl. 2.

C. 3 adds trees behind the church.

9. f. 9 *b*. II. 18. Letter to Thyatira.

Above *l*. cloud, and Christ half-length, with cross.

Below, *l*. John looks up. *c*. four people look to *r*. *r*. John facing *l*.

Below this: *l*. John with extended hand. Two candlesticks. *r*. a bedstead on which lies Jezebel in rich dress, with mitre-like head-gear.

'I will cast her into a bed.'

C. 4. (Bulletin, pl. xxix). Christ has no cross. Trees are added.

10. f. 10 *b*. III. 1. Letter to Sardis.

Above *l*. Christ as in 9: above, *deus fortis*.

Below, *l*. John writing: the inkstand on top of an upright rod beside his chair. Below him two men with spears. *r*. Angel and Church: below, three men, two with spears.

'I will come unto thee as a thief' (?)

C. 5.

11. f. 11 *b*. III. 7. Letter to Philadelphia.

Above, *l*. Christ half-length with key. *r*. door opening in heaven.

Below, *l*. John. *r*. Angel points to Church: below, eight people go towards the Church, which is approached by steps.

'who hath the Key of David' . . . I will make him a pillar in the temple of my God.'

C. 6.

12. f. 12 *b*. III. 14–22. Letter to Laodicea (1).

Above, *l*. Christ half-length with cross. *r*. a walled city.

Below, John, three men. Angel and Church.

Below this, plants: a small church with tower.

The exact point of the picture is not obvious: but the Laodicean letter is longer than the rest and perhaps required two pages.

C. 7.

13. f. 13 *b*. III. 14–22. Letter to Laodicea (2).

Above, Christ with rod touches a door on *r.*

Below, a tree, a fire: *r.* John points to *l.*

'Behold I stand at the door and knock', Schellenberg, pl. 3.

C. 8.

14. f. 14 *b.* IV. 1. The door opened in Heaven. The Vision.

Above, *l.* arched door open. Christ(?) with a roll. In an 8-shaped glory, one like Christ seated with sceptre. *r.* John in white with roll.

A band of cloud, dotted with white and smeared with white and red: undulating.

Below, the Elders, two rows of twelve nimbed figures holding rolls, seated on long benches.

C. 9.

15. f. 15 *b.* IV. 5. The Majesty.

Above, in *c.* God on circular rainbow, with roll. *r.* and *l.* the Four Beasts: *l.* Angel, and winged Lion with books. *r.* Eagles and winged Ox with books.

Below: row of seven hanging lamps.

Plants and water at bottom. Schellenberg, pl. 4.

C. 10.

16. f. 16 *b.* V. 1. The Elders adore.

Above, *l.* John, as surprised: the Book with seven sealed cords crossing it. *c.* God with roll on rainbow. *r.* Angel with rolls points down.

Below, *l.* Twelve Elders in groups of four. *r.* Twelve more in fours all hold up wreaths. Schellenberg, pl. 5.

C. vacat.

17. f. 17 *b.* V. 6. The Lamb appears.

Above, *l.* Angel over Lion. *c.* The Lamb within the rainbow, head to *l.* cross-nimbed, with seven horns and seven eyes: wound in side. *r.* Eagle over Ox.

Below, *l.* John weeping (garment held to eye). *r.* Angel points to *l.* Schellenberg, pl. 6.

C. 11. A tree between these last figures: the one on *r.* has a book.

18. f. 18 *b.* V. 7. The Lamb takes the Book.

Above, *l.* and *r.* the Four Beasts. *c.* the Lamb, the Book between his fore feet.

Below, a row of Angels with rolls, and the Elders with oblong harps, and goblets.

C. vacat.

19. f. 19 *b.* VI. 1–8. The first four Seals.

Above, the Four Beasts and the Lamb as before.

Below, *l.* a nimbed horseman with bow. *c.* an Angel gives him a wreath. *r.* John.

Below, *l.* nimbed rider bearded, with sword. *c.* nimbed rider on dark horse, with scales. *r.* nimbed rider with raised hand. Below him the spread wings and head of Hell.

C. vacat.

20. f. 20 *b.* VI. 9–17. The fifth and sixth Seals.

Above, the Four Beasts and Lamb.

Below, the Sun, a red bust in a rayed disk. The Moon. A bust in a blue disk.

Below, *l.* two Angels holding garments. *c.* a draped altar, below it *l*, four nude souls face *l.* four face *r.* *r.* two Angels as on *l.*

C. vacat.

21. f. 21 *a.* VII. 1–3. The Angels holding the winds.

Four Angels, each holds one of the Winds, represented as a half-figure with blue wings proceeding from the head, the hands joined in front of the body: the whole set in a goblet, the stem of which is held by the Angel.

C. vacat.

22. f. 22 *a.* VII. 4–8. The Sealing.

Above *l.* cloud. *r.* red sun.

Below, *l.* four Angels over 13 men in two rows. *c.* Angel with rayed nimbus. *r.* John: below him, trees, water and three fishes.

C. 12 varies the number of men and of fishes.

23. f. 23 *a.* VII. 9 sqq. The Great Multitude.

In two tiers. Above, a row of four busts of angels. Below these the Four Beasts and the Lamb (in *c.*): the Beasts are here heads with six wings depending.

Below, the Elders in two groups: under them, *l.* six men with palms face *r.* *r.* John faces *l.*

C. 13 combines nos. 23, 24, omitting the Elders and the men with palms.

24. f. 24 *a.* VIII. 1–4. The Trumpets given: the Censer.

Above, the Four Beasts (heads with two wings) and the Lamb with book.

Below, *l.* four angels with trumpets. *c.* altar: angel takes censer. *r.* three angels with trumpets: John below.

C. 13 (see above).

25. f. 25 *a.* VIII. 5. The Censer cast into earth. The First (and Second) Trumpets.

Above, *l.* angel with cross and trumpet. *r.* six angels with trumpets. Below them, *r.* angel in air, head to *l.* pours a bowl upon trees: on *l.* fire rises. on *r.* is water with two ships and fishes.

C. 14.

26. f. 26 *a*. VIII. 10–12. Third Trumpet.

Above, *l*. Moon. *r*. red Sun. In *c*. a red vertical ray ending in a star of nine rays.

l. four angels with trumpets. *r*. three.

Below, *l*. John. *r*. four dead men with rough hair: under them, water.

C. 15.

27. f. 27 *a*. IX. 1–12. The Locusts. Very little colour.

Above, *l*. Eagle. *r*. Sun. Under them *c*. four angels, *r*. three.

Below, *l*. a tree: four locusts (two-legged, otherwise naturalistic). *r*. a well-head with fire in it, a star above it. John.

C. 16.

28. f. 28 *a*. A second picture of the Locusts.

Above, *l*. a cloud: John. Before him two corpses. *r*. an angel pierces a man with a rod.

At bottom, two men and four locusts, nimbed, with human faces and long hair.

C. 17.

29. f. 29 *a*. IX. 14. The Angels in Euphrates. Unfinished.

Above, *l*. a cloud; four angels: John below. In *c*. altar, divine Hand from cloud: angel holding a chain below.

r. three angels; below, four seated angels chained by the hands.

C. 18.

30. f. 30 *a*. IX. 16. The Horsemen.

r. a cloud: John. *r*. rider with helmet, blue armour, raised sword. His horse, lion-headed, breathes fire, and has a snake for tail, which is killing a man; another man is under its feet, another in front of it suffocated by the fire.

Below, two more riders killing several men. Schellenberg, pl. 7.

C. 19.

31. f. 31 *a*. IX. 1–7. The Great Angel.

l. cloud: angel with crested nimbus and hand raised, holds a book: water below. *c*. hand out of cloud: below, a table and ink-stand. *r*. John writing and looking up. The Book is a diptych with stylus stuck into the join of the tablets.

C. 20.

32. f. 32 *a*. X. 8. John takes the Book.

l. cloud: three angels: water below. *c*. hand: angel as before gives John the Book. *r*. three angels.

C. 21.

33. f. 33 *a*. XI. 1, 2. Measuring the Temple.

l. cloud: angel gives rod to John: below, four men with crowns and disks. *c.* three similar men. *r.* temple: altar seen within. Steps lead to the door, a curtain is in the doorway.

C. 22.

34. f. 34 *a.* XI. 3. The Two Witnesses.

l. cloud: two nimbed men with rolls, the Witnesses. *c.* angel with hands extended. *r.* John.

Below, *l.* water: out of it comes the forepart of a piglike beast with lions' feet. Six men flee towards a church on *r.*

C. 23.

35. f. 35 *a.* Again the Witnesses. Unfinished.

Above, *l.* the cloud, and witnesses as before. *r.* seven angels with trumpets.

Below, *l.* six men. *c.* city falling: dead men among the ruins. *r.* John.

C. 24.

36. f. 36 *a.* Adoration in Heaven.

Above, cloud. *r.* and *l.* group of twelve Elders. *c.* the Temple in heaven: oblong, round opening in gable, curtains in side openings.

Below, John, a tree, seven men.

C. 25.

37. f. 37 *a.* XII. 1–6. The Woman and Dragon. Unfinished.

Cloud. Great coiling serpent, crested, with feathered wings, and six subsidiary heads below the topmost one. *r.* the Woman: her nimbus has stars, her hands are raised; the Sun and Moon, busts in disks, are beneath her feet.

At bottom, four men with shields and spears. *r.* John.

C. 26.

38. f. 38 *a.* XII. 7. The Fight with the Dragon.

l. the dragon, yellow and blue, falls: below him five angels fall. *r.* nine angels, two thrusting with spears. John below.

C. 27.

39. f. 39 *a.* XII. 13. The Woman pursued.

l. cloud. The dragon in air vomits water which falls into the mouth of a colossal female bust (the Earth) rising out of the ground, her head thrown back, curling hair and jewelled collar.

r. the Woman, winged, in air. John below.

C. vacat.

40. f. 40 *a.* XIII. 1, 2. The Dragon and Beast.

l. cloud, the Dragon, the Beast. Below, *r.* John and a crowd below him.

C. vacat(?). Omont's description is not quite clear.

41. f. 41 *a.* XIII. 4. The Beast adored.

l. and *r.* two crowds of men. *c.* John above: below, the Beast facing *l.*

C. 28.

42. f. 42 *a.* XIII. 11. The False Prophet.

l. Temple, the Beast seated in the porch: below, another Beast. *c.* a stream of fire descends. *r.* above, John, below, a crowd of men, and at bottom a serpent in a den.

C. 29.

43. f. 43 *a.* XIV. 1. The Lamb on Mount Sion, the Four Beasts. Divine Hand in *c.*

c. the flat-topped mount with the Lamb. Lambs on *r.* and *l.*

Below, *l.* four men. *r.* four men and John. Schellenberg, pl. 8.

C. 30.

44. f. 44 *a.* XIV. 6. The Angel with the Everlasting Gospel.

Above, angel with book, flying.

Below, *l.* crowd of men. *r.* John.

C. 31.

45. f. 45 *a.* XIV. 8–12. The Second and Third Angels.

Above, *l.* two angels. *r.* angel with book, flying.

Below, *l.* a falling building, the Beast seated in the porch. *r.* John: below, men worshipping the Beast.

C. 32.

46. f. 46 *a.* XIV. 14. The Harvest of the Earth.

Above, *l.* temple: angel flies to *r.* *r.* Christ seated with sickle.

Below, *l.* Inkstand on upright stand. John writing. Hand out of cloud above.

C. 33 combines 46 and 47 (Omont).

47. f. 47 *a.* XIV. 18. The Vintage of the Earth.

Above, *l.* temple. Angel and Christ reap off the heads of groups of men with sickles. *r.* angel comes from altar. John.

Below, three men ride to *l.* over corpses.

C. 33.

48. f. 48 *a.* XV. 1. The Vials given. The Harpers.

Above, seven angels with blue bowls.

Below, four angels on water, with fishes: four men, John.

C. vacat.

49. f. 49 *a.* XVI. 2. The First Vial.

Above, *l.* the Temple, a hand emerging. The Four Beasts half-length with cups.

Below, *l.* four angels, one pours cup upon men below. *c.* angel with raised hand. *r.* three angels with cups. John below. Schellenberg, pl. 9

C. vacat.

50. f. 50 *a*. XVI. 3 sqq. Second, Third, and Fourth Vials.

Above, *l*. four angels with cups. One pours his into the Sun, two pour theirs down upon rivers and water below.

c. altar. *r*. three angels with cups.

Below, in *c*. angel half-length in water: *r*. a crowd, John.

C. vacat.

51. f. 51 *a*. XVI. 10 sqq. Fifth and Sixth Vials.

Above, *l*. seven angels with cups. Two pour them, upon the Beast and upon a river. The Sun on *r*.

Below, *l*. John, the Dragon, Beast, and False Prophet (small, with square nimbus): each vomits a frog. *r*. three men.

C. vacat.

52. f. 52 *a*. XVI. 17. Seventh Vial.

Above, *l*. four angels with cups. *c*. Temple and Divine Hand. *r*. three with cups.

Below, *l*. John. *c*. a falling building. *r*. hail falls on men.

C. vacat.

53. f. 53 *a*. XVII. 1. The Scarlet Woman (1).

Above, angels with cups: two groups of three.

Below, *l*. John. Angel points to Woman in rich dress holding a cup, mounted on a Beast, water below.

C. vacat.

54. f. 54 *a*. XVII. The Scarlet Woman (2).

l. John, angel, woman on beast.

C. vacat.

55. f. 55 *a*. XVII. The Scarlet Woman (3).

John, angel. A river, enclosing seven men in one of its bends. The Woman with cup stands on the streams.

C. vacat.

56. f. 56 *a*. XVIII. 1–4. 'Come out of her, my people.'

l. angel flies down, John. *c*. a city: inside are three devils, nude winged figures with books. *r*. eight men face *r*.

C. vacat.

57. f. 57 *a*. XVIII. Fallen Babylon.

Above, a cloud and hand. Below, John: five men go to *l*. *c*. city: three devils in tunics sit on the towers. *r*. five men go to *r*.

C. 34 (Bull., pl. xxx).

58. f. 58 *a*. XVIII. 9. Lament over Babylon (1).

Above, John, city, men weeping.

Below, an ox, a tree; a man in a chariot, with two-lashed whip drives two horses to *l*.

C. vacat.

9. f. 59 *a*. XVIII. Lament (2).

Above, John, an angel flies down, a stone falls, the city in flames, five men weep.

Below, the sea and two ships with two men in each; two have steering paddles.

C. vacat.

60. f. 60 *a*. XVIII. Lament (3).

Above, a cloud, six half-length angels with trumpets.

Below, John, the city, men weeping.

C. 35.

61. f. 61 *a*. XIX. 1. The Triumph in Heaven.

Above, cloud, the Four Beasts with human bodies, half-length: below them in *c*. Christ on the rainbow: behind Him the Elders in groups of four.

Below, John and a crowd looking.

C. vacat.

62. f. 62 *a*. XIX. 12. The Armies of Heaven.

Above, cloud, Christ riding to *r*.

Below, crowd, angel, John writing.

C. vacat.

63. f. 63 *a*. XIX. 17. The Armies. The Birds summoned.

Above, Angels on horses. *c*. Christ rides to *r*: below them, birds flying. *r*. angel on the Sun.

Below, two hosts of foot and horse meet.

C. 36 (Bull., pl. xxxi), combines 63 and 64.

64. f. 64 *a*. XIX. 19. Defeat of the Beast.

Above, angels and Christ ride to *r*.

Below, *l*. two angels fly down to pierce the Beast and the Prophet.

c. the mouth of the pit (a well-head): birds, above, eat the heads of men. *r*. John: below him, an angel with key holds a chain attached to the Dragon's neck.

C. 36.

65. f. 65 *a*. XX. 1. The Dragon shut up. The First Judgement.

Above, six nimbed figures on thrones, a foot board runs below.

Below, eight men in two groups, an angel thrusts the tail of the Dragon down the well-mouth. *r*. John.

C. 37.

66. f. 66 *a*. XX. 9. The final defeat.

Four streams of fire fall on ten men, John. *r*. angel, his hand on the Beast who has human body, horns, and goats' head. *r*. lake of fire.

C. 38.

67. f. 67 *a*. XX. 11. The final judgement.

Above, *l.* cloud, city, three angels, one offers a book to (*c.*) Christ seated on the rainbow. *r.* three angels, one offering a book.

Below these, John, and seven nude figures.

Below, *l.* water, angel beckoning to it (to give up the dead). *c.* angel points to the severed members of a body which are to reunite. *r.* angel thrusts four men and a devil into fire on *r.*

C. 39 (Bull., pl. xxxi).

68. f. 68 *a.* XXI. 1–7. The speech of Christ.

Above, *c.* Christ. *l.* four angels. *r.* three.

Below, John writes (inkstand on *l.*). *c.* a church, six men, a fire.

C. 40.

69. f. 69 *a.* XXI. 8 sqq. The New Jerusalem.

Cloud. *l.* John and angel on a flat-topped mount. *r.* the city, circular, with embattled wall.

C. 41. The city has twelve towers, and two churches; the foundation in three bands, red, green, and blue.

70. f. 70 *a.* XXI. 15. Measuring the City.

John. Angel with rod. City.

C. 42.

71. f. 71 *a.* XXI. The City (1).

l. Four men, two holding disks or caps. *r.* the City; inside it, the Lamb with a cross, and a tree with three stems spreading widely. *r.* John.

C. 43.

72. f. 72 *a.* XXI. The City (2).

A cloud. Angel flies down. Three men below: *r.* a church with three towers.

C. 44.

73. f. 73 *a.* XXI. The City (3).

l. the city. Angel facing *r.* John, bearded, writes.

C. 45. John is bearded here also.

74. f. 74 *a.* XXII. 1. The River of Life.

A stream with plants by it flows down from *l.* into a pool of sexfoil shape. On *l.* two men, a third stoops and drinks. On *r.* a half-length angel with cross points to the water.

C. 46.

75. f. 74 *b.* A later drawing.

l. Christ. *c.* three angels adore in a horizontal posture. *r.* John with scroll.

PAGE 37. The Cycle in the Bamberg Apocalypse consists of the following pictures.

1. full page. John bearded, receives book from Christ beardless, bending out of a cloud.

2. Vision of Christ. 3 candlesticks on *l.*: 4 on *r.* The sword crosses His mouth, the stars about His hand: He holds a book. John in front on *r.*: both beardless.

3–6. A series of John and the Churches. In each the component parts are John, bearded, with book or scroll, a church, and Christ speaking out of a cloud in upper *r.* corner. Nos. 3 and 6 have one such scene only, 4 and 5 have two, and John is half length.

7. The Majesty. Mandorla surrounded by the Four Beasts (six winged). God with large cross in nimbus throned on rainbow holding roll, a sphere beneath His feet; five trumpets project downwards.

Below, *r.* and *l.* are groups of crowned Elders holding flaming horns. In *c.* at bottom, a head with water on either side.

8. Above, *l.* God throned. *r.* Elders cast down horse-shoe shaped crowns. Seven lamps hang above.

Below, angel and John with book.

9. Above, the Lamb seven-horned, stands on the book, on a throne between two six-winged seraphs.

John beardless and angel pointing up.

10. half page. 1st Seal. Rider with bow. Lamb (dark) cross-nimbed *r.*

11. half page. 2nd Seal. Rider with sword. Lamb with book.

12. half page. 3rd Seal. Rider with scales. Lamb with crown in mouth (so also in 10).

13. half page. 4th Seal. Rider with no attribute. Lamb with book.

14. half page. 5th Seal. Lamb on altar with white cross marked with small crosses. Below, robed men with pallia on their necks (stoles marked with crosses).

15. half page. Two pairs of angels half length (in two tiers), each pair back to back admonishes with the hand one of the winds which are horned busts in the four corners of the picture.

16. full page. Above, group of men holding palms. Lamb on rocky mound on *r.*

Below, John, beardless, with book, and angel.

17. half page. Seven angels with curved trumpets to their mouths.

Below, altar with crossed cloth (as in 14). Angel empties censer on earth. John, beardless, half length with book.

18. half page. First Trumpet.

Angel, below the feet parts of three spheres containing trees and hills, flaming. John, half length, beardless.

19 in text. Second Trumpet.

Angel on water with fish and overset ship. John as before.

20. in text. Third Trumpet.

Angel. Star with rays descending. Two dead men. John.

21. in text. Fourth Trumpet.

Angel. Sun, moon, stars in sky. John stands *r.*

22. in text. The Eagle.

John stands *l.* The Eagle *r.*

23. full page. Fifth Trumpet. The Locusts.

Star in cloud. Rays descend. Angel on *r.*

Below, Well head. Two crowned female-headed long-haired locusts leap out. John half length *r.*

24. full page. The Horsemen. The Angels in Euphrates.

Above, altar, cross-nimbed hand emerging from it. Angel with trumpet holds the hands of one of four half-length angels in a row, the hands of three are crossed and bound.

Below, three mailed horsemen in conical caps ride to *r.* over corpses.

25. half page. John. *l.* the great angel, one foot on water and one on land, hands him a book.

26. full page. John with rod touches the temple (small) and takes book from angel on *r.*

27. half page. Above, the two witnesses, white bearded, in robes hatched with cross lines.

Below, *l.* they crouch, a dragon leaps down on them. *r.* they stand and converse.

28. half-page. Adoration in Heaven.

l. Mandorla. Christ on rainbow with book. John below, half-length. *r.* Crowned Elders advance. Angel with trumpet above.

29. full page. The Woman with a great wheel-nimbus of sun and stars, standing in crescent holds the hand of a nude child. The Dragon, two-legged, winged, with one large snake head and six smaller, looks back at her. Above it, the Temple, and Ark in doorway.

30. full page. Above, two angels with shields and spears thrust down at two dragons, winged, two-legged, single headed.

31. full page, acanthus leaf frame. XII. The woman winged flies horizontal to *r.* Below, the seven-headed dragon vomits water upwards towards a hill in mid-air.

32. half page. The Beast with one large head and six smaller, horned; its neck maned: two forelegs and coiling body emerge from water to *l.* John *r.* with book.

33. full page. John *l.* half length. The Beast, one head, two horns rising out of water looks back to *r.* A crowd of men look on.

34. full page. The Lamb on rocky crescent. Two groups of saints above *l.* and *r.* John looks down on *r.*

35. half page. Three angels fly horizontal to *r.*

36. full page. At top, *l.* John with book. Below him, the temple: an angel emerging cuts three vines with sickle. Another angel speaks to Christ crowned seated on cloud *r.* with sickle. Divine Hand in upper corner. Ears of corn growing on *r.* below.

37. full page. Vials given, and harpers.

Above, angel gives drinking-horn to the foremost of a row of seven, who hold horns.

Below, three pairs of harpers in mantles and tunics standing on the sea.

38. full page. The first three Vials. Three angels stoop and empty the Vials. On *l.* a group of men. *c.* sea with fishes. *r.* three rivers flowing out of hills.

39. full page. Fourth, Fifth, and Sixth Vials. Three angels above, as before: the Vials are poured on (*l.*) the Sun, a dark-rayed bust in a disk, who covers his face: men below shade their heads with their hands. *c.* on three beasts emerging from earth and water; one is horned, from two of their mouths leap frogs. This combines the seat of the Beast and the frogs (Fifth and Sixth Vials). John is in the *r.* corner half length.

40. One-third page. Seventh Vial. Angel flying to *l.* pours Vial on city and sea with island.

41. full page. At top John and one angel, half length, look down over a horizontal partition at the Woman seated full face on seven-headed Beast and holding a horn.

42. full page. 'Come out of her.' Angels out of cloud above.

Below, *l.* cloud and hand with rays in form of cross projecting: at bottom. *c.* city upside down. *l.* group of men going *l.* *r.* group weeping.

43. full page. Angel standing on sea facing *l.* lets a millstone fall.

44. full-page. Triumph in Heaven. Above, *c.* Christ on rainbow in mandorla, surrounded by the Four Beasts. *l.* and *r.* two angels blow trumpets.

Below, two groups of crowned Elders. In front John crouching and an angel speaking to him.

45. Two-third page. The Armies in Heaven.

Above, three horsemen ride to *r.* The foremost has diadem, sceptre, and sword crossing his mouth: the third a whip.

Below, Angel blowing trumpet. John half length. Two birds of prey perched on two crowned men and devouring them.

46. full page. Defeat of the Beast. Above, three warriors thrusting downwards, the one on *r.* bends from his horse.

Below, *l.* a flaming rock. On it lie the dragon and nude Satan with rough hair, coupled by an iron band. Satan's wrists are crossed and bound by a ring, and his ankles fettered. *r.* two men shelter themselves from the sword of the horseman above.

47. full page. Satan imprisoned. Satan and the dragon coupled together are pushed by an angel on *r.* to a flaming rock on *l.*

Below, a winged rough-haired devil holds the bonds of Satan and the dragon whose necks are ironed together and Satan's wrists are in an iron ring. Behind them is a flaming rock.

48. full-page. Last judgement. Conventional form. At top, *c.* Christ throned supporting a large cross. *l* and *r.* rows of half-length angels, two with trumpets.

Just below *l.* and *r.* two groups of six seated Apostles.

Below *c.* two angels with scrolls, Uenite benedicti etc and Discedite a me maledicti &c. Below their feet men rise from coffins.

l. group of blessed, one in pallium. *r.* another group of cursed, one in pallium. Two trumpet angels at the sides.

In *l.* corner John. In *r.* corner Satan with chained wrists and ankles, and a devil taking hold of the lost.

49. full page. The New Jerusalem. Above, an oval of battlemented walls and four groups of three towers. Within it the Lamb standing on a roll or cushion.

Below, Angel with rod pointing up takes the hand of John on *r.*

50. full page. The River of Life. At top, in *c.* Christ throned with extended hands: a half-length angel on each side. From the base of the throne a stream flows downward to *l.* Three trees grow on the ground on *l.* Between them John kneels towards an angel on *r.*

PAGE 38. The subjects of the Beatus cycle will be found described in the following publications. Frimmel, l.c., p. 41; the Turin MS.; Delisle, *Mélanges d. archéol. et de paléogr.*; the MS. from S. Sever, at Paris; James, *Fifty Manuscripts* (H. Y. Thompson, 2nd Series), no. 97; the MS. of 894; *Rylands Library Cat. of Western MSS.*, no. 8; Astorga-Didot MS. See also K. Miller, *Die älteste Weltkarten*, 1895, pl. i, and Neuss, *Die Katalanischer Bibelillustration*, where much is said of other copies, notably those of Gerona and Urgel, and many illustrations are given.

In the same very important volume (p. 131) an account is given of the illustrations of the Apocalypse in one of the two great Catalan Bibles, those of Ripoll ('Bible of Farfa' at the Vatican) and of S. Pere de Roda (Bible de Rosas or de Noailles, Paris B.N. lat. 6). Only the latter contains any Apocalypse pictures, and these, it is notable, do not derive from the Beatus cycle, but resemble far more nearly that of *Trèves*. So says Neuss, but I am not struck by the likeness. They represent

1. The Vision of Christ in 8-shaped glory. 4 candlesticks on *l.*, 3 on *r.*

2–8. A series of the Letters to the Churches, each consisting of John addressing an angel, a small church between them.

9. A large drawing of the Vision of ch. iv. and the Adoration of the Lamb. Two moments are shown. Above, is God in mandorla surrounded by the Four Beasts (six winged). Elders throned on *l.* and *r.* Lamps hang from the bottom of the mandorla. Angel and John are on *l.* Below, the Lamb with cross and book, in a circular halo, the Four Beasts below: *l.* and *r.* angels and elders adore.

10–13. The Four Riders. The fourth has a devil below him. These like 2–8 are small drawings inserted in the (triple) columns of the page.

14. The Fifth Seal. Souls lying and standing: above, the altar and Divine Hand.

15. The Sixth Seal: Sun, Moon, falling stars, men hiding in caves on hills.

16. The Angels and Winds. They stand above and below a central circle and each holds a human head, winged. A larger angel below on *r.*

17. The Trumpets. Above, God in mandorla: four angels with trumpets on *l.*, three on *r.* Below, the Lamb with cross, in a circle.

18. The angel takes censer from altar.

19. Angel blows trumpet. 20. Angel with trumpet. Star falls. 19, 20 are unfinished, and no more illustrations occur.

In these pictures John is beardless.

PAGE 39. The Apocalypse picture in the Bible of Charles the Bald is divided into two tiers. In the upper is the Lamb about to take the Book and the Lion of Judah facing him on *r.* The Rider with the bow is seen over the Book. The Four Beasts are in the angles.

In the lower half is in *c.* a figure without nimbus, bearded, throned. An angel blowing a trumpet is before him. The Lion is on *l.* Ox on *r.* Eagle overhead. This human figure can hardly be God, says Frimmel, but the man-figure of Ezekiel's vision; but

I doubt this. In the upper corners are *l.* John weeping and the Elder pointing to the Lamb: *r.* John taking the book from the great angel (ch. x) who stands on sea and land, represented by two heads.

In the Bible of St. Paul's is a picture in three tiers: in the upper and lower are the Seven Churches with their angels: in the middle, the Lamb and Book on the altar. God throned on *r.* and the Four Beasts.

The Alcuin Bible corresponds with that of Charles the Bald.

The codex Aureus of St. Emmeram, at Munich (Cimel. 55) has a fine picture of the Elders adoring the Lamb. Earth and Sea are represented by figures below.

The Mosaic at Aix-la-Chapelle was a Majesty with twelve only of the Elders offering their crowns. It was figured by Ciampini, *Vet. Mon.*, ii (1747), pl. 41.

PAGE 39. The Fleury cycle is known from the verses printed by v. Schlosser, *Quellenbuch f. Kunstgesch. d. abendl. Mittelalters*, p. 184. The order in which they are given is:

1. The great angel (x) — two lines
2. The death and revival of the two Witnesses (xi) — four lines
3. The angel (or eagle) crying Woe (viii) — two lines
4. The locusts coming out of the pit (ix) — four lines
5. The Adoration of the Lamb (v) — ten lines, elegiac
6. John beholding the souls of the martyrs (either v. 9 or xx. 4) — two lines
7. Measuring the temple (xi. 1) — two lines
8. The two Witnesses (xi. 7) — one line
9. The birth of the child and flight of the Woman (xii) — three lines
10. The fight with the dragon (xii) — two lines
11. The angels in Euphrates and the horsemen (ix. 14) — six lines
12. The birds devour the slain (xix. 21) — three lines
13. The ark seen in heaven (xi. 19) — two lines
14. The first judgement, by the Saints (xx. 4) — three lines
15. The beast and Satan emerge after the thousand years (xx) — two lines
16. The final resurrection (xx. 12) — ten lines
17. The new Jerusalem (xxi) — two lines
18. Hell — four lines

The true order seems to be 5, 6, 3, 4, 11, 1, 7, 8, 2, 13, 9, 10, 12, 14, 15, 16, 17 (18).

PAGE 48. With regard to Paris fr. 403, it may be well to call attention to a note of Cent. xv which is at the bottom of f. 1, and has (for a wonder) been wrongly interpreted by M. Delisle. It is:

> fiat opus abstractum Costesey et Hugo de vi super apocalipsim, et inscribatur circa et sub picturas sequentes et tunc erit complacens, et si necesse fuerit fiat rasura gallic'.

Delisle reads 'Costesdy' and interprets 'Costeby', but the real name is that of the Franciscan Henry of Costessey or Cossey near Norwich who died in 1336, and was a writer of some note. Several MSS. of his commentary on the Apocalypse exist, e.g. Laud. Misc. 85 in the Bodleian. A remarkable commentary on the Psalms survives in a single copy at Christ's College, Cambridge. Hugo de Vi I take to be the well known Hugo de Vienna (or de S. Caro) who commented on the whole of the scriptures. Delisle suggests H. de Vitonio or de Virley.

The intention, then, was to disfigure the pages of the MS. by the insertion of a more up-to-date commentary in Latin, and if necessary to make room for it by erasing the French text; an intention happily, as Delisle says, not carried out. There are instances, e.g. in the Cambrai MS., 482, of a long commentary being added on intercalated leaves, which is a comparatively harmless process.

The note in fr. 403 is in an English hand, and will have been written while the MS. was in this country, in the possession of the Duke of Bedford.

LECTURE II

PAGE 59. The Paris MS. B. N. lat. 10474.

It has the stamp of the Jesuit College of Lyons: Ex Biblioth. Pub. Colleg. Lugdun.

Former owners' marks are: (*a*) on the fly-leaf 'Villeneufue' (xvii–xviii).

(*b*) In an elaborate frame painted on the fly-leaf: Noalhes (xvi) with monogram below.

(*c*) On p. 47 *b*. Pierre(?) de Noalhes and

Celuy ou celle qui ledit liure retrouuera
a ledit Pere(?) de Noalhes le rendra
et sil ne luy rend
Le Diable lenportera incontenant. P(?) de Noalhes.

(*d*) the late name Lenoir.

On 48 at top is a monogram of IHS (xv) in Gothic letter and below it a poor drawing (xv) of Christ on the Cross and the sun and moon: apologies for figures of Mary and John have been added. All this might be English work.

Text, in double columns of 19 lines, the text of the Book in larger script than that of the gloss. At first the script of both is pointed and seems to be by one hand: later, that of the gloss is rounder, but that of the text seems uniform throughout, as if a first hand had written all the text and begun the gloss, and another had completed the gloss. Yet sometimes the large script of the text is used for the gloss and vice versa. This is also the case in *Douce*.

On p. 22 the section of text is first referred to as an Epistola: the page ends: et cetera ut in epistola sequenti.

On p. 46 is the first displacement of a piece of the gloss. The note is: 'quoniam glosa huius epistole hic finem suam facit, congruum est sumere de glosa epistole sequentis que nondum ibi finitur propter artitudinem loci', and accordingly p. 45 ends: 'et cetera ut supra'.

p. 53 ends: 'Et quoniam in precedenti epistola glose ratio nequibat terminari, hic diffiniuimus'. A single clause follows, supplementing the last words of 52.

p. 54 ends: 'et cetera ut infra', and on 56, col. 2 is: 'Possumus hic de glosa epistole tercie antecedentis (i. e., p. 54) (sumere) ad huius columpne spatium adimplendum que sic accipitur'.

p. 77 ends: Glosa huius epistole et proxime sequentis una est.

p. 78 ends: Inuenietis residuum glose in epistola sequenti.

p. 79, col. 2 has: Glosa epistole antecedentis hic adimplebitur secundum quod huius columpne spatium potuerit sustinere, que talis est.

p. 82, col. 1: 'Hic additur de glosa epistole octave subsequentis (in fact p. 88) propter nimiam huius columpne ⟨breuitatem⟩ et consequentis prolixitatem, que sic accipitur.' I think *breuitatem* is obviously needed. *Douce* has the same note and the same omission.

p. 85 ends: 'et cetera ut in quarta epistola subsequenti' (i. e. 87, col. 2).

p. 86 ends: 'glosa huius epistole ab eiusdem auctore inuestigata in hoc loco finem suum facit', which seems to be mere padding.

p. 87, col. 1 ends: 'Residuum glose istius epistole quere in vi[a] epistola que antecedit'. The reference should be to p. 82. In col. 2 is: 'Hic additur de quarta epistola antecedenti' (i.e., p. 85).

On p. 90 the whole of the two columns is occupied by text, which, contrary to custom, is carried on into p. 91, col. 1, and the new section does not begin until 91, col. 2.

The text of the Book is finished on p. 93 and a piece of gloss added, ending abruptly. The picture has not been put in, and a wretched sketch is the substitute: the last page (47 *b*) has the retrograde image of the same text.

Comparing these anomalies with *Douce* we find that though the script of the text in *Douce* is larger, that of the gloss is smaller and closer than in *Par*, so that *Douce* often has more matter. Taking the corresponding pages, 21 *Douce* (=22 *Par*) ends at an earlier point.

47 *Douce* (=46 *Par*) has the same note: but the added gloss has 14 more lines than *Par*.

53 *Douce* (52 *Par*) has: 'quia glosa huius epistole hic terminatur, ideo de glosa precedentis epistole ad implendum columpnam hic additur que sic accipitur.' 8 lines follow.

54 *Douce* (52 *Par*) ends at an earlier point. 54 *Par* is wanting in *Douce*.

78 *Douce* (75 *Par*) and 79 *Douce* (76 *Par*) have no similar notes.

80 *Douce* (77 *Par*) has the same note.

83 *Douce* (80 *Par*) has the same note, also omitting *breuitatem*.

86 *Douce* (83 *Par*) ends at an earlier point.

87 *Douce* (84 *Par*) continues into 85 *Par* and has an extra piece of gloss, not in *Par*.

88 *Douce* repeats part of 87 and omits half of the text of *Par* 85 (viz. Rev. xxi. 9*b*–10).

An omission common to the two books is this: in xvii. 15, 16 (*Douce* 73, *Par* 70) they read: 'Aque quas uidisti et bestiam hii odient fornicariam': thus omitting (after 'quas uidisti'): 'ubi meretrix sedet populi sunt et gentes et linguae. Et decem cornua quae uidisti in (bestia).' The homoeoteleuton of *uidisti* is the plain cause, but the mistake will have been made in the parent MS.

I think it is clear that the same scriptorium gave birth to *Douce* and to *Par*.

I now give a list of the pictures in *Par*, with notes of the correspondence with *Douce* (*D*) and also with *Perrins* (*P*).

Par.	*D.*	*P.*
1. John on Patmos: the Islands named	1 (reversed)	3
2. John and the Churches	2	4
Leaf gone with the Vision of Christ	3	5
and Letter to Ephesus	4	*vac.*
3. Letter to Smyrna	5	*vac.*
4. To Pergamus	6	*vac.*
5. To Thyatira	7	*vac.*
6. To Sardis	8	*vac.*
7. To Philadelphia	9	*vac.*
8. To Laodicea	10	*vac.*
Leaf lost with Vision of Heaven	*also lost in D.*	6
and Adoration of Elders	—	8

Par.	*D.*	*P.*
9. John consoled by the Elder	11	7
10. The Lamb and the Elders	12	9
11. The Lamb takes the Book	*lost in D.*	10
The Lamb adored: not in Par	*lost in D.*	*vac.*
12. The First Seal	13	11
13. The Second	14	12
14. The Third	15	13
15. The Fourth	16 (the Rider is Devil)	14
16. The Fifth	17	15
17. The Sixth	18	16
18. The Angels hold the Winds	19	17
19. The great Multitude	20	18
20. The Seventh Seal. The Trumpets given	21	19
21. The Censer cast into the Earth	22	20
22. The First Trumpet	23 (all seven angels present)	21
23. The Second	24	22
24. The Third	25	23
25. The Fourth	26	24
26. The Eagle flying in heaven	27	25
27. The Fifth Trumpet: the Locusts and Abaddon	28 The Locusts	26
	29 Abaddon	
28. The Sixth Trumpet: the four angels are demons	30 (they are angels)	27
29. The Horsemen	31	28
30. The Great Angel: The Thunders	32	29
31. The Book given, and eaten	33	30
32. Measuring the Temple (no worshippers)	34 (worshippers)	31
33. The Two Witnesses	35 (adds the olive trees and candlesticks)	32
34. Death of Witnesses They lie dead	36	33
35. People rejoice over them	37	34
36. They rise and ascend	38	35
37. The Seventh Trumpet	39	36
38. The Temple in Heaven	40	37
	41 Adoration scene	
39. The Woman clothed with the Sun	42	38
40. The Dragon: the Child caught away	43	39
41. War in Heaven	44	40
42. The Dragon cast into the Earth (unfinished)	45	41

Par.		*D.*	*P.*
43.	The Woman, the Dragon, the Flood	46	42, 43
44.	The Seed of the Woman fights	47	44
45.	The Beast out of the Sea	48	45
46.	The Beast and the Dragon	*vac.*	46
47.	The Beast adored	49	47
48.	The Beast slays the Saints	50	48
49.	The False Prophet: he calls down fire	51	49
50.	The False Prophet marks men	52	50
51.	The Lamb on Sion	53	51
52.	The Throne and the Harpers	54	52
53.	The First Angel	*lost in D.*	53
54.	The Second Angel	*lost in D.*	54
55.	The Third Angel	55	55
56.	*Beati mortui*	56	56
57.	The Harvest of the Earth	57	57
58.	The Vintage	,,	58
59.	Angels with Vials	59	59
	Harpers on the Sea of Glass	,,	60
60.	The Eagle distributes the Vials	60	61
		61	
61.	The First and Second Vials	62	62
		63	63
62.	The Third Vial	64	64
63.	The Fourth	65	65
64.	The Fifth	66	66
65.	The Sixth	67 (Kings from the East)	67
66.	The Frogs	68	68
67.	The Seventh Vial	69	69
68.	The Woman seated on the Waters	70	70
69.	The Woman on the Beast	71	71
70.	The Drunken Woman	72	72
71.	The Fall of Babylon	73	73
72.	'Come out of her'. The Lament	74	74
	Par omits xviii. 12 Merces auri–17 *a* tantae diuitiae. D *omits only* 14 *b*, 15 *a*.	75	
73.	The Merchants lament	76	*vac.*
74.	The Millstone cast into the Sea	77	75
75.	The Triumph in Heaven	78	76
76.	The Marriage of the Lamb	79	77
77.	'Worship not'	80	78
78.	The Armies of Heaven	81	79
79.	The Birds summoned	82	80
80.	The Battle with the Beast	83	81

Par.	*D.*	*P.*
81. The Defeat of the Beast	84	82
82. The Dragon imprisoned	85	(*the rest wanting*)
83. The First Resurrection	86	
84. Satan comes forth again	87	
85. The Attack on the Holy City	88	
86. The Judgement	89	
87. Behold I make all things new	90	
	91	
88. The New Jerusalem	92	
	93	
89. The River of Life	94	
90. 'Worship God'	95	
91. *text only, no picture*	96 (without are dogs)	
Par omits xxii. 16 *a* Ego Iesus–ecclesiis	97 Conclusion	

LECTURE III

PAGE 69. A list of the subjects of the Angers tapestry may not be unwelcome.

The asterisk indicates the presence of a figure of John as spectator, usually on *l.*, in a doorway.

I. 1. Large figure, under canopy, reading.

2. John (bearded). The seven churches, in two rows, surmounted by their angels.

3. The Vision of Christ and the candlesticks. John prostrate.

4*. The Majesty and Elders.

5. Angel. John. Elder consoles John.

6*. The Elders adore God.

7*. The Lamb and Four Beasts: Elders, in four compartments. John on *l.*

8. Lost.

lower row. 9*. The First Seal. The Rider with the Bow. Angel in air.

10. Lost.

11*. The Third Seal. The Rider with the Balances. Lion in air.

12*. The Fourth Seal. Death as the Rider, followed by Hell which is shown as a building in two stories. A demon above, Hell-mouth below. Eagle in air.

13*. The Fifth Seal. Souls (clad) kneeling in front of altar.

14, 15. Lost.

II. 16. Large figure lost.
17. Lost.
18*. The Majesty, with the Lamb, and the Great Multitude.
19*. ,, ,, The Trumpets given.
20*. ,, ,, The Censer.
21*. The Censer cast into earth. The First Trumpet.
lower row. 22. Lost, except the figure of St. John.
23*. The Second Trumpet. Ships destroyed.
24*. The Third Trumpet. The star falls: men die of drinking the bitter waters.
III. 25*. The Eagle. The Fourth Trumpet: fall of city, &c.
26*. The Fifth Trumpet. Abaddon &c. come out of the abyss.
27*. The Sixth Trumpet. Armed and robed angels in Euphrates,
lower row. 28*. The horsemen kill men.
29. John forbidden to write. The great angel.
30. The book given to John: he eats it.
IV. 31. Large figure under canopy, reading.
32. Measuring the Temple: no worshippers.
33*. The Witnesses call down fire and turn water to blood.
34*. Death of the Witnesses: the Beast, with a demon mounted on his back, crushes the hand of one.
35*. They lie dead. People and city on *r.*
36*. They rise and ascend: earthquake.
37*. The Seventh Trumpet. God in the sky: the Elders on *r.*
38*. The Woman: the Child caught away: the Dragon below.
lower row. 39*. Michael &c. defeat the Dragon.
40*. The Dragon pursues the Woman, to whom wings are given.
41*. The Dragon casts out water: the woman flies away.
42*. The seed of the Woman fight the Dragon.
43*. The Dragon: the Beast out of the sea.
44*. The Beast, the Dragon, and worshippers.
45*. Men adore the Beast and Dragon.
V. 46. Large figure under canopy, reading.
47*. Worshippers: the Beast: God in the sky.
48*. The False Prophet (lion-headed) beside the Beast, calls down fire.
49*. The False Prophet: men are slain: others adore the Beast on *r.*
50*. The False Prophet marks men: horsemen approach from *r.*
51*. Angel in sky: two groups of seated men.
52*. The Lamb on Sion. Four Beasts in clouds: people *r.* and *l.*
52*. Angel proclaims the Gospel. The Elders in Heaven adore the Lamb.

lower row. 54*. Angel in air with scroll: falling city.

55*. Third Angel, on earth: the Lamb beside him: people on *l.*: angels on *r.*

56*. Beati mortui. John writes: people lie in beds: above, their souls received.

57*. Harvest of the Earth: angel commanding it on *r.*

58*. Vintage of the Earth commanded.

59*. Vintage: a demon: river of blood, horses, and city.

60*. Angels harping on the sea of glass: others above in clouds with Vials.

VI. 61. Large figure under canopy reading.

62*. Lion distributes the Vials.

63*. The First Vial poured on earth.

(The Second Vial poured on the sea is omitted or lost.)

64*. The Third Vial poured on rivers: angel at altar.

65*. The Fourth Vial poured on the Sun.

66*. The Fifth, on the throne of the Beast, and the Sixth, on Euphrates: the Kings from the East are seen.

67*. The Frogs proceed from the mouth of the False Prophet &c.

68*. The Seventh Vial: God in the sky: falling city below.

lower row. 69. John is shown the Woman seated on the waters.

70. An angel carries him to see the Woman seated on the Beast.

71*. Babylon falling: men flee.

72. Lost.

73. A fragment. The woman lies in fire: Elders adore.

74. Lost.

75. John writes: is forbidden to worship the Angel.

VII. 76. Large figure, lost.

77*. The armies of heaven on *l.*, the Beast &c. on *r.*

78*. The armies: defeat of the Beast: birds in the air.

79. Lost.

80*. Saints seated to give judgement.

81*. The Beast, &c., emerge to attack the city on *r.*

82, 83. Lost.

lower row. 84. John. Christ in the sky: the New Jerusalem descending.

85. John, the Angel, the new Jerusalem.

86. John, the river and trees of life: God and the Lamb in vesica.

87. A fragment of John and Angel.

88. A fragment with angel, and Christ in glory.

89, 90. Lost.

PAGE 72. Of no. **43** the Escorial MS. a few details may be given. It is of largish size with 49 leaves: text in double columns in Latin, with the Berengaudus gloss and beginning with 'Piissimo Caesari'. The pages are bordered, which is unusual, and the pictures are half page. John, beardless, is usually outside the picture; in the latter part of the book he stands in a panel made in the border. There are 97 or 98 pictures, those on ff. 1–26 (52 presumably) are by Jean Bapteur (1428–35), the borders being apparently by Perronnet Lamy throughout the book, and coeval with Bapteur's pictures: while the remaining pictures were added by Jean Colombe of Bourges in 1482.

I have seen illustrations of the following subjects. In *Museo Español de Antiguedades IV* is a coloured reproduction of the Adoration of the Dragon who is seated under a porch-canopy.

In *L'Arte IV* are two pages, one of Colombe's work showing Babylon, a magnificent city, and the angel in air commanding God's people to leave it: the other of Bapteur's showing the seven churches as a row of seven porches of varied forms, surmounted by angels: John is outside on *l.*

In *Zeitschrift für Bildende Kunst*, 1929 (F. Winkler) are reduced reproductions of nine subjects, viz.:

1. John, landed on Patmos, opens the door of his house. There is a landscape, and a ship full of men on the sea.
2. John consoled by the Elder. The Lion of Judah with the Book is in a vesica: an armoured angel stands on *r.*
3. The Rider with the sword. The Lamb is in a vesica on *r.*
4. The Rider with the balances, facing the spectator.
5. The Rider of the pale horse, as Death, holding a mass of fire.
6. The Fifth Seal: a draped altar with chalice, paten, and book, a number of nude souls before it, and three angels robing them.
7. The Fifth Trumpet: the Star and Key in the air: Abaddon mounted rising from the abyss. On *r.* men are pursuing Death up a mountain: 'they shall desire to die and death shall flee from them'. This is unique in my experience.
8. The Great Angel. On *l.* outside the picture sits John, who is forbidden to enter. On *r.* is a scene of a preacher in a pulpit and his audience.
9. Part of the picture of the woman receiving wings and fleeing.

The last pictures as described in the *Museo* represent the raising of Drusiana, the story of Atticus and Eugenius, the drinking of the poison, and the death of John.

The work is evidently extremely fine, and though it as evidently follows the old cycle, additions are made such as those specified above in nos. 7 and 8, which are due to the artist or his director.

PAGE 72. List of pictures in the MS. Paris B.N. fonds néerlandais 3.

The pictures are in every case full page bordered with conventional clouds. Two artists seem to have been employed.

I. Scenes from the life of St. John.

At top, within a circular enclosure bounded by a low wall, a cruciform church with central spire, aisles, flying buttresses, pinnacles, and polygonal apse. On the spire, below the top, is a flag with a cross.

In a pulpit on the wall facing the W. door John beardless addresses a group of people with their backs to the church. Within the south transept he is seen baptizing Drusiana.

Below on *l.* a building with stepped gable: a robed man with staff of office stands in the door: before him is John between two guards. In *c.* John nude in a stone vat, a man on *l.* treads on bellows which work on a beam suspended to a gibbet. Another stirs the fire. On *r.* in the doorway of a rich building stands the Emperor.

In front below is a river with a bridge over it. John is in a boat between steersman and rower. On *r.* the stern part of the same boat with steersman is seen going to *r.* The first boat shows John arriving at Rome: in the other he is departing for Patmos.

Flowers and grass are on the hither bank.

II. ch. i. John on Patmos. The Vision.

Below on *l.* a man pushes off a boat from the land: on *r.* John reclines and an angel flies down with a long scroll.

Above, first the candlesticks set in a rough half-circle: then John on his knees. Christ stands with sword across mouth and open book in his hand. *l.* hand above John's head.

The Churches, aisled and apsed, some with central, some with western turrets, each with a kneeling angel in its doorway, are arranged three on either side of Christ, one above and behind Him.

III. ch. ii. Letters to Ephesus, Smyrna, Pergamos, Thyatira.

In the centre Christ, as before, with the candlesticks before Him.

Behind and above Him is a Church and two are on either side.

The first Church is otiose. To each of the others an inscribed scroll points. Each has its kneeling angel.

Top *l.* *toter kerken van ephesien.* Before this church is a group of three friar-like men, tonsured, surrounding a hooded man with a long beard who may represent a false apostle or a Nicolaitane (ii. 2, 6).

l. below, *toter kerken van smirna.* A group of five people, four of them in hats with central peak, arguing: perhaps 'they that say they are Jews and are not', ii. 9.

top. *r.* *toter kerken van pergamo.* A building with an opening and a grating below: in it two people. Outside a devil, hairy, speaks to them: 'the devil shall cast some of you into prison' (applies really to Smyrna, ii. 10).

below *r.* *toter kerken van thiathire.* A man and woman in bed. 'I will cast her into a bed, &c.' ii. 22.

IV. ch. iii. Letters to Sardis, Philadelphia, and Laodicea.

At top is a large cross-nimbed head of Christ with angels on clouds on either side. Below it a white dove flies to John who sits immediately below writing on a long scroll on his knee.

On *l.* are two churches. On *r.* one with angels in the dome: no scrolls.

Above *l.* Sardis. Below it two skeletons: 'thou hast a name that thou livest, and art dead', iii. 1.

Below *l.* Philadelphia: a group of people kneel at the door. 'I will make them to come and worship before thy feet', iii. 9.

Below *r.* Laodicea. A naked woman standing, a naked man seated with joined hands raised, another in prayer, with a cloth cast about him, 'wretched and miserable and poor and blind and naked', iii. 17.

V. ch. iv. *l.* John climbs a flight of steps: an angel in a porch at top.

c. above, a great vesica: God throned with sceptre and open book: the Four Beasts about Him: a row of seven lamps at top. Background of Elders in subdued colour, with crowns, harps, vials.

The vesica is supported by an angel with back turned to spectator, raised arms, and peacock's wings. Water with flowering plants in it in middle distance.

VI. ch. v. Lamps at top. Two vesicas overlapping. In the upper, the Lamb on hind feet at the throne: God turning to *l.* Outside on *l.* an angel apparently counting on his fingers.

In the lower, the Lamb with cross, staff, and flag, the seven-sealed book open. He has here the seven horns and seven eyes. The Four Beasts with open books surround this vesica. Outside on *l.* the Elder speaks to John. Background of Elders as before.

VII. ch. vi. The first six Seals. John sits on *l.* midway up. In an upper band are *l.* black sun, below it the Four Beasts in a row.

c. the altar with souls beneath it: on it a book, chalice, and candlestick. *r.* Head of Christ, blackened moon. Stars.

Below this, the Four Riders, the fourth being Death, with Hell-mouth behind.

At bottom, men hiding in the earth and (*r.*) a castle with door and turrets falling.

VIII. ch. vii. Above, vesica with God and the Lamb, surrounded by the Four Beasts. Background of Elders.

Lower on *l.* an angel with a cross (the seal of God) and at his feet a nude infant surrounded by rays. Below this an Elder speaking to John.

In *c.* the earth with a belt of sea and ships and cities. Four angels hold the wind-faces.

r. a group of kneeling saints.

At bottom a series of groups: from *l.* a woman(?) with a bundle of faggots. An armed man points up to Earth. Another armed man threatens a white-robed man kneeling in the door of a church: a man gives two loaves to a beggar: a house; a heap of coins in the door, a man takes some(?): a man climbs a tall ladder. A head of Christ is near the top on *r.*: a woman speaks to a naked man: a man beside a donkey. Above this a baptism, with a third figure by a church gate(?).

These are very obscure.

IX. ch. viii. At the top *r.* and *l.* an angel gives trumpets to seven angels. *c.* God throned with open book: below His feet the altar (souls seen below). *l.* angel with censer.

Below this four demi-angels blow trumpets. On *r.* eagle with seals and on *l.* angel casts censer into earth. Hail or fire falls. Stars fall. A third part of sun and moon is darkened. At bottom John seated by waters in which men are perishing. Others in terror on *l.*

X. ch. ix. At top *l.* fifth trumpet blown: great star.

Head of Christ. Altar.

r. angel with sixth trumpet.

Below *l.* hell-mouth and locusts issuing: two robed angels.

r. Four angels in Euphrates, in plate armour.

At bottom, *l.* John seated. *c.* Troop of lion-headed horse. *r.* men adore idol in temple (ix. 20).

XI. ch. x. At top in a circular glory, God throned with open book: in the circle of the glory are seven heads (the Thunders). Background of angels.

Below, the great angel robed, with crossed stole, and rayed face. He hands the book to John on *r.*

On *l.* John sits with scroll. Two angels in air *r.* and *l.* address John.

XII. ch. xi. At top *l.* John takes measuring reed from Christ (half length) from whose mouth fire descends. On *r.* above is the temple, and a nimbed figure in it thrusts out one who falls headlong. Below this a group of crowned Elders adoring (busts).

Below on *l.* the Witnesses white robed supported by two angels.

Below this the Witnesses before Antichrist.

Farther down, Antichrist is being crowned. At bottom the Witnesses are beheaded.

On *r.* an angel blows a trumpet.

A portico and Antichrist seated in it. Outside, several men about a chest in which is money and plate.

At bottom, Antichrist prostrate, a devil on his back.

These episodes are borrowed from the First Family cycle.

XIII. ch. xii. At top the woman with starry crown, surrounded by rays, the moon at her feet, reclines. An angel, from temple on *r.* takes the Child.

Below *r.* The woman winged. An angel.

The Dragon vomits water. Stars fall.

On *l.* above, Michael and an angel fight the Dragon.

Below, the winged woman among trees.

XIV. ch. xiii. At top, head of Christ.

Below, *l.* John. *r.* the Beast on the waters and the Dragon meet.

Below *c.* the Beast adored. *r.* He and his men fight the Saints, tonsured and white-robed with cross-banner.

At bottom *l.* the False Prophet with ram-horned wolf head. He presents people to the Beast on an altar without a shrine.

r. he holds a vessel and marks the forehead of a king: a clerk and a bishop wait.

XV. ch. xiv. God throned on vesica: the Four Beasts. Background of Elders. In front the Son seated, with sickle.

l. the Lamb on Sion adored. *r.* the temple.

l. a falling city. *r.* angel reaping.

l. John writes. *c.* the Beast on an altar adored. *r.* the Vintage. Horses wade in blood. The city gate on *r.*

XVI. ch. xv. A row of angels with vials.

A row of angels with harps.

The Temple. The Lion on *r.* gives Vials to angels.

John reclines. Rocks.

XVII. ch. xvi. At top, seven demi-angels empty vials. Fire and hail fall.

Below, the Beast and worshippers. Groups of men in terror. Falling city. Men perish in waters.

XVIII. ch. xvii. At top. *c.* head of Christ. *l.* angel carrying John.

r. the Lamb gives cross-shield and cross-staff with banner to two kings.

c. the woman on the Beast, on water.

At bottom, troop of kings advance from *r.* and attack the woman crowned who is in flames and holds a cup.

XIX. ch. xviii. At top. *c.* head of Christ.

l. angel lets fall a millstone. *c.* kings with scroll look up. *r.* angel holds a bird of prey by the wings.

Sea with ships. *r.* Babylon falling: people come out of it: a devil is in it. *l.* a group of kings and others look on.

XX. ch. xix. At top., *c.* God in vesica: the Four Beasts.

l. at table, the Bride and the Lamb and guests. *r.* angel in the sun, birds below.

l. John addressed by angel. *r.* the Army of Heaven attacks the Beast and his men—the Leader's garment spotted with blood.

l. men driven into hell-mouth by a devil. *r.* the Army pursues them.

XXI. ch. xx. At top, *c.* the Judge in vesica, crowned witn thorns and showing His wounds. He holds two swords, the points at His mouth. *r.* and *l.* groups of seated saints. A double rainbow below the Judge's feet.

c. man rising. Hell-mouth on *r.*

l. angel with chain and key: the Dragon enters a prison-door.

c. He emerges with men, and attacks the city on *r.*

XXII. ch. xxi. At top, half length of Christ with orb.

l. angel in air with measuring reed and vial. John below. *l.* the New Jerusalem. Circular towers at angles, each with one of the Four Beasts in it. The sides each consist of three ogival crocketed arches apiece, an angel in each. In the city is the Lamb with flag.

Below are kings bringing golden vessels.

XXIII. ch. xxii. At top, God throned and the Lamb. Background of angels.

l. Angel supporting John. *c.* the River of Life and trees on either side. *r.* the angel. John below, about to worship him.

PAGE 74. The subjects prescribed for the illustration of the Apocalypse in the *Painter's Guide* are:

1. The Vision of Christ, i. 9.
2. The Lamb and the Book, iv. v.

3. The first four Seals, with the Riders, vi.
4. The Fifth Seal, with Souls under the altar, vi. 9.
5. The Sixth Seal, with mountains falling, vi. 12.
6. The Angels hold the Winds: the 144,000 are sealed, vii.
7. The Great Multitude, vii. 9.
8. The first four Trumpets, viii.
9. The Fifth Trumpet, with the Locusts, ix.
10. The Four Angels in Euphrates: the Horsemen, ix. 13.
11. The Great Angel and the Book, x.
12. Measuring the Temple: the two Witnesses, xi.
13. The Seventh Trumpet: the Adoration in Heaven: the Hail, xi. 15.
14. The Woman (represented as the Virgin): the Child born: the Dragon pursues, xii.
15. The Beast out of the sea, and the False Prophet, xiii.
16. The Lamb on Mount Sion: the Fall of Babylon, xiv
17. The Harvest and Vintage of the Earth, xiv. 14.
18. The Seven Vials, xv, xvi.
19. The Woman mounted on the Beast, xvii.
20. The Fall of Babylon and the Triumph in Heaven, xviii, xix.
21. The Armies of Heaven: the Defeat of the Beast, xx.
22. The Beast cast into the pit, xx.
23. The great White Throne and the Judgement, xx. 11.
24. The New Jerusalem, xxi, xxii.

INDEX OF LIBRARIES

Roman figures refer to the list of Early Cycles (p. 21). Arabic (in italics) to the main list.

www.ingramcontent.com/pod-product-compliance
Lightning Source LLC
LaVergne TN
LVHW020642100826
845148LV00012B/2301

9781666734959